My Mountain Granny

The Story of

Evelyn Howell Beck and the Mountain Town of Whittier, NC

by Matthew Link Baker

Catch the Spirit of Appalachia, Inc.
WESTERN NORTH CAROLINA

Best wishes!
Matthew J Baker

SECOND EDITION 2009

Photos & Map: Stuff & Such, Whittier, NC • Layout/Edited by Amy Ammons Garza
Interviews & Sources: Doug Revis, Gene Reid, Ed Martin, William Wike, Jack Game
Wilma Ashe, Bill Lewis, Evelyn Beck, Terry Howell, The Heritage of Jackson County, NC, Vol. 11

Publisher:
Catch the Spirit of Appalachia, Inc.—Imprint of:
Ammons Communications — SAN NO. 8 5 1 – 0 8 8 1
29 Regal Avenue • Sylva, North Carolina 28779
Phone/fax: (828) 631-4587

Thank you to the North Carolina Arts Council and the Jackson County Arts Council,
who funded, in part, the publishing of this book through a Grassroots Arts Program.
Contact Number: 828-293-3407

Thank you to Catch the Spirit of Appalachia, who also assisted in the publishing of this book.

Library of Congress Control Number: 2009928856
ISBN: 978-0-9824099-2-3

Dedication

I dedicate this book to Evelyn Howell Beck. Evelyn was one of the finest human beings one could ever meet. She allowed a young college student into her home and treated me like family. I learned lessons from her that could never be taught in a classroom.

There were no layers to be peeled away when meeting Evelyn. She was a hard working woman who lived her life by the light of faith and love of family. I am thankful to her for memories of our friendship. She had a story to tell, and my job was to write it down. It is my hope that you will enjoy her story as much as I have enjoyed writing it.

The Beginning

Coming to the mountains as a young college student, the land fascinated me. I had expected the place to be suspended in time, but I soon found the mountains changed drastically from what I had imagined. I had expected the country store. Instead, I found Wal-Mart. I became curious and wondered what old Appalachia was really like. My desire was to know the mountain people, not as popular culture portrayed them, but for who they really were.

For some time my curiosity led to nothing. I had begun attending a writing group, and one day I started talking with a lady by the name George-Anna Carter.

"I'm interested in talking to someone about the old times," I told her.

"I know just the person you want to talk to," she said, and scratched a name and number on a piece of paper. I rushed home and dialed the number. The lady and I spoke, talked for a little while and then arranged to meet the next day.

On December 10th, 1998 my adventure began, for the moment I met Evelyn Howell Beck I knew she was special.

Evelyn and I visited on different occasions. At first it was awkward. I had grown up with MTV and she with square dances. In fact, we had nothing in common except that we were fascinated with each other.

Soon after I began visiting, my questions began to be answered. I had found a mountain woman who had lived Appalachia's history.

I always took a tape recorder to our visits and had lots of questions. If it was winter, we'd sit out on the porch in front of the stove. When the conversation died, we had the crackle of the fire. On several occasions during the summer we'd take walks around the campground or take short trips together. What started as an awkward meeting, became a unique friendship. Neither of us made sense of it until, one day, Evelyn summed it up, "I guess I'm just your Mountain Granny."

In truth, she was much more than that. An amazing history of fantastic people and places was revealed to me, but most of all I had found a role model. I regret not telling her this while she was living. I was young and could be told nothing. Here I had found someone who didn't need words, a person who had lived her faith...and I failed to let her know my feelings! In many ways just knowing her changed my attitudes about faith, family and life.

Now, years after her death, I have her story and the memories of our friendship. What I've written is not a novel or a story of my own doing. My task as writer was to stay out of the way. The story was already written with the evidence of the life of Evelyn Howell Beck. I've only added little bits of information, where relevant, and kept it just as she told it.

What follows is the culmination of a dream for me, one that changed my life and gave me memories that will last a lifetime.

—Matthew L. Baker

View of the original town of Whittier, Swain County side of the Tuckasegee River. Today only the Whittier Hotel still stands (center, left of the Baptist Church). c. 1880's.

SETTING OF STORY: WHITTIER, NORTH CAROLINA
A Lumber Town Founded by the Cousin of Poet John Greenleaf Whittier

Founded in 1885 by Clark Whittier, cousin of poet John Greenleaf Whittier, this town was built around a stop on the WNC Railroad and fueled by the timber boom of the late 19th century and early 20th century. Whittier grew quickly, and by 1913 boasted a drug store, a hotel, sawmills, lumberyards, more than a dozen stores, three churches and a school. The Depression, the decline of the demand for lumber, and the founding of the Great Smoky Mountains National Park caused a decline in Whittier, and in 1933 the townspeople petitioned the state legislature to revoke the town charter. Today Whittier is a pleasant village consisting of a post office and several businesses.

Contents

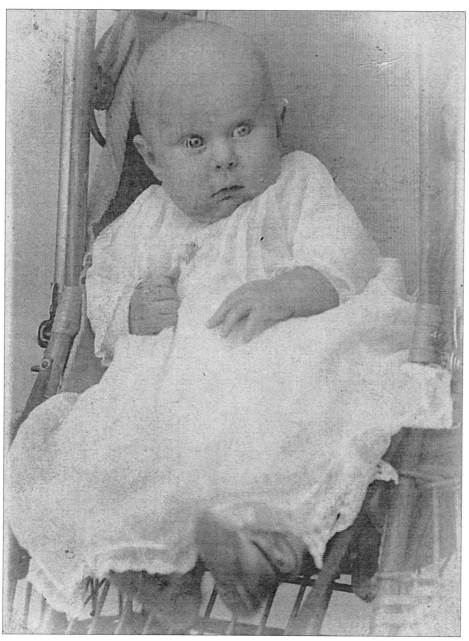

Baby Evelyn
Born June 26, 1917

Chapter 1
CHILDHOOD STORIES

"Hello, Evelyn, how are you?" I ask as she lets me in.

"Well, I had about give you out. I've missed you. Come in."

Typically she'd be fixing something to eat and she'd offer to feed me.

"Now what do you want to eat?" she asks.

I'd always tell her ham, plain, with no tomato. She'd fix the sandwich with tomato, and most times, I'd just remove it and not say a word.

"How's that little wife of yours?" she asks. "I want you to bring her to see me."

Evelyn often asked about my little wife, for I had brought her with me on one occasion. I had been attending a history lesson, one that my little wife had no interest in, but had come with me because she wondered why I made the trips to Whittier so much.

"Let's sit down out here by the fire," she says. "Do you have any questions for me today?"

"Yes, I do," I say.

This time, Evelyn surprises me and begins reading one of her own writings.

"I want you to know what it was like for me to grow up in the little town of Whittier, N.C., where I was born on June 26, 1917. It was a mighty nice place for a child to live. I had the best childhood of anyone I ever knew."

"Whittier was just a small town then. But we children had a lot going for us. We all had to work a lot doing chores before we could play. Then, our group of about eight girls would go to town and to the stores to hang around. We had a lot of ball games in our gymnasium, plays and other things. We'd go swimming in the Oconaluftee River. We had a real good swimming hole over there. We'd bunch up a big crowd of us and go over there when it was real hot. The water felt so good, especially if we had been picking

My Mountain Granny

blackberries all morning. Our mothers canned them and made jelly and jam."

Did you have a lot of friends you played with?

"Oh, yeah, I had a lot of friends. Everyone liked me, and I had a big sense of humor. I laughed a lot, because things were funny to me. I'd get tickled and I'd laugh."

Did your mom and dad let you go over to other friends' houses to play?

"They gave us a time to come back when we went to visit. Our friends' mothers would tell us when it was time to go home. I was never allowed to play with boys. It's a wonder I ever married, but I married at 17 and my sister Edna married at 18. We played outside and built playhouses in the woods. We had no special toys...for it was an innocent time. We thought the biggest crime in the world was for someone to get drunk. I look back on that and think that I didn't have a care in the world. There were always old drunks that sat around the stores all day. They didn't harm nobody.

"We had a swimming hole over at the Oconaluftee River in Birdtown. Our mamas let a bunch of us girls go swimming all day long. We'd pick black-berries all morning and head to the river in the evening—it's a wonder we didn't drown."

Did you get into trouble much?

"I never did nothing real bad. One Sunday evening, we sneaked into the neighbor's house and got her broom and dishpan. We then fixed a playhouse in the barn-loft. Lord, we had the best playhouse that evening. When our mamas called us, we went home. When we got home and ate supper, Corey came walking along. I can see her plain as day. She's a coming down the road with her hands in the air yelling, 'I been robbed, I been robbed!'

"Our mamas gave all four of us a whipping with a hickory switch and switched us till we carried every-thing back to Corey's. We wasn't going to hurt her stuff, we was just borrowing it.

"But I tell ya, when I grew up, the young folks had to make their own fun, and they had good times. I know I was bad not to go where I told mama I was going, but I never told her a story. Of course, I never took nothing because it was stressed in us—if it doesn't belong to you, don't mess with it."

Did you ever get an allowance?

"Lord no, our parents didn't have nothing to give. We would go to the riverbank and pick up liquor bottles the old drunks would throw away. Along the riverbank was where we'd find batwing bottles which was a little flat liquor bottle. We'd look for the batwing bottles, bring them back to John Revis, and he would give us a five-cent piece for two. That's how we had money to get into the ballgame that night.

"It never dawned on me that John was selling liquor. He was one of the kindest men that ever was in the world to us youngin's--we was all crazy about him. He was just a kind and Godly man, even if he did sell liquor. He was good and kind-hearted to us youngins. He was a good man to everybody. He kept many a person from starving to death during that Depression. If they didn't have a dime of money and needed bread, they got it.

"The Civilian Conservation Corps boys had their ball games in our gym at school. We didn't have no nickel, so John bought our bottles and we'd get to go to the ballgame. The three CCC camps would come to play in Whittier's gym. Of course, with all the CCC boys there, us girls naturally wanted to go to the games. In times like that, you learned how to ease around and get what you wanted. Really, we were happy people. If we were the only ones who didn't have anything, that would have been bad, but nobody did, so we were all in the same boat.

"My uncle was co-owner of the big Roane and Varner store. I can show you right now where they had bananas that hung on the stalk. I can remember standing there looking up and wanting one so bad. I didn't have any money, and I didn't get one. People bought just what they had to have."

So you had never heard of TV?

"We'd never heard of such things because we made our own entertainment. We liked playing all kinds of ball, and in the winter we played card games. I look back now and realize that was happy times. I didn't have a care in the world."

My Mountain Granny

What did you dream of doing when you were little?

"I think I wanted to be a nurse. We had a little hospital in Whittier. There were two nurses there, and I envied them so much. I never got to be one, but my daughter did. I married at 17, so I had no chance to get trained."

Did anything strange happen when you were a kid?

"I remember when Wilbur John Smith died. It really frightened my sister Edna and me. Wilbur John had been the neighborhood eccentric. He lived in a two-story home and to my knowledge, it had never been painted. He would storm and shout at all the children as they walked by his house. My sister and I would run by his house, snickering and laughing at him.

"All our elders said that when he died, he would come back and haunt us. I believed what they said, so you can imagine the fear I felt when he died. Somehow the bright idea popped in my head to get

Wilbur John before he got me. My sister said, 'If you stand over your worst enemy's grave and chant Voodoo three times, the so-called enemy could never touch or haunt you from the other world.'

"Somehow that made sense to my ten-year-old mind. I asked her if she knew the Voodoo words. She answered, 'Of course I know the words.' We practiced saying the words on the way to the cemetery and soon found Wilbur John's freshly-dug grave and bright, shiny tombstone. We both stood trembling and looking down on it. My sister knelt down and tried to say the magic words that would wipe Wilbur John out of our minds forever.

"Wouldn't you know, she tried and the words wouldn't come out. I knelt down beside her, and try as I might to help her, I couldn't say them either. Then, something strange happened—the earth shook, thunder rolled loudly, and the wind started blowing. My sister and me found ourselves running as fast as our legs would take us toward home. Even now, sixty years later, every time it storms, I try to think of the Voodoo words just to get even with Wilbur John."

Chapter 2
CHORES

cinating about history. It not only teaches us about society's gains but also its losses. In some ways, to discover the future we need to rediscover the past.

—Author

It was very valuable to me to learn what chores were about in the old days. Growing up in the 80's, I never set foot in a garden. I thought that grocery shelves had roots, and that was where food came from. I had little things to do around the house, but I didn't grow up working as Evelyn did (I grew up in "Good Times," as she often called it). My childhood was something those in Evelyn's day could never have imagined.

Children nowadays do not have what Evelyn had. Sitting in front of the TV just doesn't build character in the same way as having the responsibility of helping keep the house clean or feeding the farm animals. Wouldn't it be great if more value was placed on simple chores so children will value what they have, as Evelyn did in her day? That's what's so fas-

Evelyn, what chores did you do when you were little?

"When I was growing up in the little village of Whittier, I had to help do all of the chores. As I got older, I did more chores and harder ones. I had to help my mother make the garden each Spring. She took me with her when I was small. I was too little to plant and hoe, but she fixed that. She handed me a pail and said, 'Go fill the pails with cow manure for I am making cucumber and tomato hills.' I carried pails and pails of cow manure, and I never forgot. We'd never heard of fertilizer, and I don't think anyone had any. That was the end of my farming. I didn't like it then and don't like it now!

"But, oh Lord, I had to hold the wood when

daddy sawed. Daddy didn't have a boy, and I was the one he would take outside to help him. When I got big enough, Mama and Daddy let me hoe.

"It seemed Mama never could do nothing with me and daddy could. I bucked her on everything, and I don't know why. I know one time I wanted to say 'Damn.' I'd know to get to the door before I said anything that would bring Mama's wrath. I'll never forget that one day, I looked back and said, 'When I grow up I'll say 'Damn' if I want to.' I thought it was over. When I came back, she had a big hickory laying on the table about that loooong. I want you to know she trimmed my legs and I didn't say 'Damn' no more.

"Edna worked more inside than me. See, Daddy didn't have a boy, and anytime he needed something held or something done, he'd take me since I was older. Edna had to do the dirty work...what few things there was to do."

Didn't your family do a lot of farming?

"You couldn't go to the store and buy nothing, so we farmed and raised what we necded. I was always helping. I never did learn how to milk a cow.

14

Mama tried to teach me. When I couldn't do it, she boxed my jaws and sent me to the house a'crying. I tried, but I did it...like this way, and back like that. I never did learn, I guess I was afraid of the cow. I can't milk to this day.

"We lived out in Qualla until I was about 5 years old. My younger sister and I were playing one hot summer day while Mama was helping Daddy hoe in the field. Anyhow, I stripped off my baby sister and set her down in the spring. She just screamed real big and loud. Mama switched me for that but I was cooling Edna off.

"I got more spankings than Edna did because I was a different kind of child. Edna was quiet and when she got hurt she'd get off to herself and cry. I'd just talk back and get more spankings. When my brother came along he was just like me. He would talk back to the president!

" I remember one time Edna went to vote and they made her write her name to prove she could write. I told her, 'He thought he'd knock you out of voting because you was Republican. Why I would have hit him in the face,' I told her. 'Why you're crazy! I wouldn't have written my name for him. No way!'"

Chores

So he handed her a piece of paper and asked her to write her name?

"Yeah, I wouldn't have done it! I would have said, 'NOOOO! I ain't about to write my name.' I'd have had to hit him and then let the law get me for hitting him but she didn't and she was mad about that for ages. The man who pulled that on her was an old Democrat and I knew him all of his life. Edna married a Republican and voted with her husband, while I married a Democrat, and I voted with my husband. Edna would let people do her in and go off and cry about it. I was a rowdy little girl, and my sister was so shy and quiet. Some little girls would hurt her feelings and she'd come crying to me, 'So and so done something to me,' and I'd go tearing into them. I got in trouble several times when I'd come back at my teachers. I'd get punished and they'd make me stay and write something 100 times.

So you were not one to back down?

"Nooooo boy, I didn't back down! I held my hand with whatever I had to hold it to. I led Edna into everything. We'd do all kinds of things, not real bad

Evelyn and Edna as young women

things, but things Mama didn't want us to do."

"We lived right on a paved road, and I remember my sister and me learning to skate on it. We got down below the house where Mama couldn't see us and went to town on them roller skates. This old man we called Uncle Pouty saw us and told our mama. I didn't like him anymore after that. There weren't many cars passing, but Mama put a stop to our skating. She throwed our skates in the river and I can still hear them, plunk, plunk, in the river. That broke my

15

heart because, if she had left us alone, we could have made good skaters."

What other things did you and your sister do for fun?

"The main pastor at that time, down here in Whittier, had three little girls about me and my sister's age. He had a car and there weren't many cars at that time in Whittier. He came by in the summer and got my sister and me to take us to the Oconaluftee River to go swimming.

"To get away from the house, Edna and me slipped off because Mama wouldn't let us go. We went swimming, to ballgames, and dances. From the house, we could hear the music, and away we'd go. There were some of the prettiest dances. The men came from Haywood and brought a band. Sam Queen always came and called the dance. I loved to dance the old-timey square dance."

How old were you when you learned to swim?

"I learned to swim while Daddy bathed in the river."

16

Did you and your sister get along?

"I got along well with my sister. She was easy going and had a calmer nature while I was hyper.

"One time we got the measles. Why, I was right fair-skinned and, Lord, I went to breaking out before I knew that I had them. My sister was darker-skinned and she was really sick. Dr. Tidmarsh would stop every day and check her and I'd be in the bed over from them. He'd say, 'I'm not gonna look at that one. Ain't nothing wrong with her.' Mama made us stay in the bed while we was broke out. I got out one day while Mama was fishing and played Hopscotch. She came out there in the yard when she got home, and boy she got me back in bed."

What is the most favorite memory of your childhood?

"You didn't have much going in recreation cause during the Depression no one had any money. There were some kind of happenings in Asheville with the railroad. They ran the train to Asheville. I remember there was a dance sponsored by the railroad, and I

Chores

was so thrilled to get to go. Daddy took my sister and me on the train because he worked for the railroad and could ride free. When we came back, it would be 12 or 1 at night. The railroad had it for their employees. That was the biggest thing in my life at the time."

What about a memory of your brother?

"I wrote this for my brother. It's called, "To Brother—Neurotic.
I didn't do that...I hadn't touched a thing that belongs to you, and I'm not going to be accused of it. I haven't done it, so don't you say another word, or I'll slap your face into kingdom come. Now do you hear me, smarty?"

"My brother encouraged me to buy land beside the house. We bought the land, and I still own it. Mack was the cause of it, for I would have bucked my husband. I didn't want to turn that money loose. Mack said, 'If you don't do that, you're crazy as a loon. Give me that offer, and I'll buy that land. I own from the driveway of the next house and plumb up on the mountain. Nobody can get any closer to me than they are."

"My husband knew what to do. He just came in here and called Mack, who was a surveyor. He's dead now but good gracious alive he knew land.

"Me and him would fuss like everything. He'd turn around, hand me a twenty and say, 'I'm giving you this.' I'd say, 'Mack, I don't want your money.' He was the best thing in the world to me.

"His wife, Denna, was just like a sister to me. After Mack died, Julius was done in the home and Denna lived in Bryson City. Lo and behold, she and her mother went down to Georgia to see her sister. They had a car wreck, and both were killed. It's a thousand wonders I hadn't been with them that day because she'd call me and want me to go places with her. That came within one inch of killing me because that was the last family that I had. I still can't cope with that good yet. I've been through some pretty hard knocks in my life, but I come through it all."

It made you stronger going through it, didn't it?

"I guess so. Now I don't fly up and fall over nothing. I don't do that."

Chapter 3

LIFE AT HOME

You were born in 1917, right Evelyn?

"Yes, I was born in 1917, and I'm gonna have a birthday soon, before too long, on June 26. I've had lots of birthdays, and I've enjoyed every one of them. In fact, I just kind of enjoy life, to tell you the truth."

Did you and Edna share the same bedroom?

"Yeah, not the same bed, but the same room. See there's just about seventeen months between us. Well, we had a dresser and a bed. We had all we needed in there. Of course, back then nobody had anything fine around here. It wasn't like that. They had just what they needed."

Your mom sewed didn't she?

"Yeah, she sewed all the time. She sewed and she made things for people. She had a sewing machine and she'd make dresses and things for a lot of women who had girls and couldn't sew. Now, I never did master that, but she sewed and that helped during the Depression. She made money to buy material to make us dresses. I had a good childhood, really I did.

"Mama was tall, and she had coal black hair. When we was little, mine had a red tint to it when I was in the sun. After I got older, it turned dark."

Back then they wore long dresses, didn't they?

"Pretty much, yeah, and Lord, you never heard of a woman wearing pants. I'd even go pick blackberries with a dress on. It was much later before women started wearing pants. I can remember back when things were so different.

"All of Daddy's people were strong

Life At Home

Republicans, and Mama's family were Democrats. I hated Herbert Hoover, and I couldn't stand to look at his picture when he was in the paper. I'd punch a hole in it and say, 'I'll never vote an old Republican ticket." Daddy never would say a word to me. Till I'm as old as I am, I've voted a Democratic ticket. I blame Hoover for all that Depression. I'm sure now that he wasn't to blame for all of it. I was a very determined kind of person. I set my head about something, and it was that way.

"Daddy was Baptist, and I never saw him in a Methodist church. Mama was a Methodist, and I never saw her in a Baptist church. Daddy was a Republican, and Mama was a Democrat. They went out every election and voted a straight ticket. Daddy would take me to church one Sunday and Mama would take Edna. The next Sunday Mama would take me and Daddy would take Edna. Mama would go to the Methodist church and on Election Day she'd go out and vote a Democrat ticket and Daddy would go out and vote a Republican ticket. They could have just as well have stayed home. I never did see them have words over that. No way in the world...I never did. I thought what in the world will I be—a Republican or a Democrat, a Baptist or a Methodist? Mama and Daddy never tried to influence us either way...they left that to us.

"I really liked the Methodist Church better than the Baptist, but I went to the Baptist Church because my husband was of the Baptist faith. Some of the members had yard parties in the summer. They played games in the yard and had lemon cake and things to serve us. Well, that was a big treat for us youngin's. Little things like that didn't cost nothing. We had a lot of social life in Whittier.

"Mama made us get up early. We ate breakfast together as a family. Mama would bang on the wall and say, 'Get out of there!' Daddy would leave for the job. They had a depot in Whittier then. The railroad workers met there and then rode to Dillsboro and their territory. There were about five men in his crew. When that Depression came, he finally got laid off."

What was one thing your parents tried to teach you?

"Oh, they tried to teach me, but I'd sass them. I don't know what made me do that, but I did. Lord, that would just kill my mama. Mama would talk to me about that. She'd say, 'Evelyn, be kind and don't sass.' That was the most she ever got on to me about anything. I'd sass the teachers in school, too.

Were your mom and dad the biggest influence in your life?

"Both of them did but I lean a little more towards my daddy's people than I do my mothers people, about thinking and doing."

Was prayer a regular thing in your home?

"Daddy always said grace before eating. Lots of nights before we went to bed, Daddy read the Bible."

How did your parents meet?

"Mama's family lived on Camp Creek and Daddy's family lived on Shoal Creek. Daddy rode a horse, and they met at church. Imagine that; courting riding on a horse."

Evelyn's father and mother, Harley and Myrtle Howell, riding in a horse and buggy in 1913 during their courting days

Did your parents ever give you a nickname when you were little?

"I didn't have a nickname until my brother was born. He couldn't say Evelyn, so he said Ebbie. He called me that a long time until he could talk good. My name is Harriet Evelyn. My grandmother, Varner, was

Standing front Row on stepway (L-R)

| Garth Reed | Rachel Conley | Edith Varner | Louise Whisenhunt | Dorothy Rhodes | Reva Debord | Beatrice Styles | Maureen Ashe | Edna Howell |

Seated (L-R)

Middle Row (seated L-R)

Seated (L-R)

| Green | Martha Varner | | X | Clayton Davis | Daniel Childers | | Haven Davis | Everett Bass | Hall McLean | X | Lucile Styles | Ethel Rogers | Madge McHan |

Standing (L-R)

Back Row (L-R)

2nd Row (L-R)

| Ruth Kerlee | Jennie Redmond | Evelyn Green | Howell | Dorothy Redmond | Eugene Gibbs | Teacher Hazel Crawford | Hilliard Mathis | Ted McLean | Raymond Gasaway | Lee Wilson Dunlap | Robert Varner | Dorothy Patton | Myrtle Davis | Ernestine Gibson |

1926-27 School Year

21

My Mountain Granny

named Harriet Varner. I don't know where they got Evelyn from."

What was one thing in particular that your parents tried to teach you?

"Mama always said, 'Behave yourself!' That was a big thing for me when I was young. I was full of devilment. Mama would say, 'Be a lady—shut your mouth.' I got lots of switchings because I'd sass and talk back. I was good to mind but I'd talk back or die. When my youngun came along, I thought, 'Lord, I hope she's not like me.' Joyce never was one bit sassy."

Tell about Christmas when you were young.

"My daddy believed in buying apples and oranges, probably down at Roane's. My sister and me always got a new doll and a storybook. Sometimes Daddy would buy a box of peppermint stick candy. We'd hang up stockings over the fireplace and I really believed in Santa Claus."

Roane & Varner's in the 30's

Chapter 4

OLD-TIME RELIGION

I've been thinking about sounds. I love to hear many different kinds of sounds around me and don't appreciate a very quiet period. Our lives are made up of all kinds of sounds, large and small. We prefer pretty to ugly in most things in life. There are many beautiful sounds that we can hear. Most of the time I like soothing music, birds singing, and crickets, but I love to hear bells like the ones at churches.

"Where I grew up in Whittier, there were four church bells within my hearing range. Each bell had a different sound or tone. I remember listening to each one and I could recognize the church by the sound of the bell. As a child, I would pause and listen to each one welcoming people to the church doors. It was a good sound and I think perhaps it was one of the most beautiful sounds that I've ever heard. The ringing of the bells carries a good feeling for me and has stayed in my memory for a long time," Edna shared.

You've seen a lot of changes. If you could give advice to the younger generation on dealing with change, what would it be?

"I always felt that if it wasn't something I could change, accept it. Some things I could change and I did, but you don't change everything. That was kind of my philosophy. I never have been a big worrier...it wastes energy and it tears up your mind. I don't particularly like living up here by myself at all, but I can't change it. I'm just as happy as I can be here. I'm thankful I've got a roof over my head, food and a car I can drive. I get to studying about all the things that I have and think, 'What's the use in dwelling on being by myself.' There's no point in that and I certainly can't bring my husband back.

"I guess the first thing I'd say is get your faith anchored in a higher power. Do that and the rest will

My Mountain Granny

fall into place. There's so many that don't even believe and I think that's so tragic.

"Well, let me tell you. There's enough of that writing in the Bible to know how to live right and be decent. Of course, I've studied the Bible for years and years. Now I've been to church all my life, and I'm a' getting old. I've heard every preacher that's ever been in this country. I've heard them all, and I sum it up: 'Trust in the Lord and do the right thing.' The Bible says 'Believe in the Lord Jesus Christ and you shall be saved,' and that's a verse of Scripture. I've come to that time and time again. When you believe, you're gonna try to live to please him. Don't go off on some foreign worship somewhere. Now down at our church the preacher preaches too long and I've got out with him. He don't know when to hush. He won't come by to see me, but if he does come to see me, I'm gonna tell him!

"He's young, and I'm gonna say, 'Listen, I've been in church all my life, and I've learned a little bit along the way. Cut your messages down, and you'll have a bigger congregation. I could help him, if he'd let me, but he knows it all. Now we had one pastor and every one loved him better than anything in the

24

world. Twenty minutes and he could tell more than any of them could tell in forty minutes. Twenty minutes and he was out of that pulpit just like that. He stayed with it a long time and I hated for him to leave. Now these big long messages: I ain't gonna set for no more, because I've done enough of that in my day.

"As old as I am, I pretty much know God's Word. I pretty well know what a preacher is gonna say. My mother was old-timey Methodist, Daddy was Baptist and my brother was Presbyterian. My sister and me were Baptist. I have been going some lately to the Methodist church down here in Whittier. My uncle: he gave land for the church and gave part of the money to build it. My family's names are all over the windows."

Do you have a family cemetery?

"Well now, that one on Union Hill is kind of like a family cemetery. That's where Julius and his parents are buried, and that's where I'll be buried cause I got the stone and won't leave that for Joyce to pay for. Funerals are a big racket these days. Lord, that's the biggest in the world."

Whittier Missionary Baptist Church

This is possibly the oldest church in Whittier. Today a stone church has replaced this original wooden structure.

The house on the hill to the left was the home of Sebron (Seab) Varner. It no longer remains.

My Mountain Granny

I heard about a man who had cancer but he had decided before he died that the family would have the funeral in the house. They did it all by themselves. They even dug the grave themselves.

"Well, used to, that's the way people done. They had them in the homes back when I grew up. My husband was put away real nice...nothing elaborate. We didn't live that way and I don't believe in dying that way."

My wife and I have talked about being cremated.

" I can't stand that. My granddaughter comes up with that to me every once in a while. 'Granny, I'm gonna be cremated, and if I ever live here I'm gonna see that you're gonna be cremated. I say 'Don't you see I'm cremated.'

"Me and her get into it over that. I say, ' Don't you talk to me, because I don't believe in that.' I say, 'that's an old heathen custom. Read your Bible, the Egyptians and all those old heathens done that back yonder.' I say, 'No, I ain't gonna be in that.' She just does that to get me started but she don't believe in it. Back when I grew up everybody that was anybody at all went to church. Now some ole socks and things, there was always some of them around, they didn't go to church.

"I've always been bad to get tickled in church. My mama used to have trouble with me. I'd get tickled in church and she'd just want to whip me all over. 'Evelyn quit giggling, quit laughing in church.'

"I been going lately to this little church and you know it's so handy there. The pastor, his mother was a nurse at the health department and I worked with her. He's the pastor; Lord, I've known him all his life. I go down there and it tickles me to death. He hugs my neck and just loves me cause I've known him all of his life. I can walk right over there and I know everyone there. They are all local people and they're so sweet and friendly."

Chapter 5
I REMEMBER WHEN

Did you make your soap?

"Mama made soap, and it was just as white as could be. She would cut it into big blocks. That's what we washed our clothes and everything in homemade lye soap.

"One time I told my grandson about that, and he laughed at me. He can't imagine that, because he's been raised in good times. I said 'You ain't never took a bath till you take one in old homemade lye soap.' One time you had to have soap and couldn't get none. You had to have a bath and we used that soap. Jerry thought that was the funniest thing in the world, me taking a bath in old homemade lye soap. He can't comprehend a Depression , cause he came along in such good times. We had one bath tub, and we washed off once a week. Now, peoples got to bathe everyday but back then people didn't do that. We sponged off the rest of the time. Everyone done that because you couldn't bath everyday. You didn't have running water, but people then were as healthy as they are now."

Did you travel in a buggy?

"Whenever we went to the store then, we went in a buggy. There for a while, that was the only way they had of going to the grocery store or anywhere. From here, we went up to Wilmont and back. We loved to travel on the back roads. Lord, I remember that our horse's name was Sue. I remember that just so well. Oh, we'd also go to church in the buggy. We went to trade with the horse buggy back then. People liked to take one day and fill the back of a buggy with stuff. I remember that just so well, although it seems like it's been a hundred years ago."

My Mountain Granny

Early days of Whittier— 1908

Tell me about washing clothes in the old days.

"We did that on an old rub board. When I got old enough, Mama made Edna and me do that. Lord, that blistered my fingers, and the next time, it wouldn't be healed up. That didn't make a bit of difference to Mama. She put us right back at it. We boiled the clothes in a big old black pot. The clothes had to be

boiled cause there wasn't no such thing as Clorox. I don't think they had Clorox then and boiling the clothes was the way Mama disinfected the clothes.

"That was before electricity came and we had flat irons. We'd heat them on the stove and iron with them. Lordy day! Whew! Yeah we had a big old ironing board and it paddled good.

"We had to scrub floors. People didn't have

28

Whittier in the 1930's

floor covering then. They just had floors. You kept them scrubbed just like everything you did. Well there was a whole lot of things to do. I swept the yard, and later we began to get grass yards. Back then everyone had dirt yards, and we kept them swept, oh, so clean. Mama always had pretty things a'blooming outside."

Do you remember any of the herbs your mother used to use?

"Oh, gosh, I can remember ole yellow root tea. Lord, she gave that for everything that got wrong with us, and it must have worked cause we got better. It was bitter as everything, but Mama was a big believer in that. Where we lived, she'd go way up Ingle Branch, and there was a lot of yellow root there. She'd go up there and get that and make that old yellow root tea. She'd make me and Edna drink that. It was bitter as everything. I hated that, but I always got better."

My Mountain Granny

Who had the first car in Whittier?

"Perby Bennett had the first one. He owned the first drug store, and he had a car. His son still comes to our class reunion because I graduated with him. He had the little Ford Roadster, and I can remember us getting out here and going around looking. We thought that was the prettiest little thing we had ever seen, but he had the only car on that hill. I remember that just as well. He was so down to earth. Lord, when we go to the class reunions, he comes and puts his arm around us and loves us all. He said, 'Lord, there's so few of us left. We're so glad to get to be here today.' He's one of the nicest fellows you'll ever meet. He's retired now, but we had a good time even if it was during the Depression.

"We didn't know what a car was. There wasn't none, and I can remember the mailman that went on the route with the horse and buggy. We didn't live on a route. We lived in Whittier. The mailman went out on Route One and Two through Qualla. It would take him all day to make the run with the horse and buggy. John Green was his name, and Lord, he's been dead years, but I can remember that so well.

"Whittier was just a wonderful little village. Lord, us kids could play in the road all day and never get run over. There wasn't anything to run over you. We played ball games and everything in the road."

Where did you go when you got sick?

"Dr. Tidmarsh lived in Whittier all his life, I think. He knew everyone personally, and if you got sick and didn't have the money, he would see you anyway. Lord, everybody liked Dr Tidmarsh. Lord, I remember him coming in a horse and buggy. In a way it was hard times, but in a way it was good times."

Did you have a radio in those days?

"The first radio I ever saw was in Roane and Varner Store on the big wide steps. They set the radio in the middle of the steps and everyone came to hear the radio. I was about nine years old and there was this old fellow there named Uncle Hamp Woods. We were setting a'listening to the radio, and I was all ears. He kept on saying, 'I thus don't believe a word of that.' Well, that tickled me. I giggled and giggled over that, and he still didn't believe it.

"We got our first radio after Julius and I were married and our first TV after moving onto Conley's Creek.

"John Revis had the only phone in Whittier. John was good to everybody and they would go over and use John's phone."

When did you get electricity?

"We didn't have electricity till I lived in Whittier on Shoal Creek, just before Julius went into WW II. Oh, I thought that was the grandest thing in the world. We had an icebox, and the man used to bring us ice during the summer. We bought a refrigerator and then a stove. Little by little, we got it all. A dollar and a half was our first electric bill."

When did credit cards come along?

"We'd never heard of such a thing—we'd never heard of a credit card. The only time I got a credit card was the time my daughter and me decided to take a trip to Florida. Instead of carrying money, I decided I might better get a credit card. When I came back, I paid it off, and that's the last time I had one. I never have been much to go in debt for nothing. I waited till I got the money and bought what I needed."

Evelyn told me what she remembered about Whittier.

"In a way, I lived in a hard time during that Depression but people were good. They believed in the Lord and believed in doing the right thing. They believed in the right thing more than they do now. It was harder about money, but morally the people were good moral people. Now we had one or two old drunks that hung around in Whittier, but they were about all that was there. They were good-hearted, never said a curse word to us in our presence and weren't dishonest. They were just drunk. We kids just danced around their knees. When I grew up, there weren't many that drank. One of them I especially remember. He was married and was a WW I veteran who was drawing a pension. This was during the Depression and we didn't have no money. He gave us a nickel lots of times to buy a Coke.

"They had square dances where John Revis store is at now. It was almost beside of where we lived. There was a pool hall and they moved the pool tables. There was good music: fiddles , guitars, banjos. They were some of the best. They really knew their music. Mama never let me go to dances, but I'd slip off and go. Mama would think we were at church.

Revis Store in the '80's

Whittier

"Rile Ingle was the hatefullest man that ever lived. Nobody could stand him, but he liked me. Once, when I was laid up on my back , he would come and see me. I'd say, 'Lord, Rile, I'm ruined.' He'd tell me "Good God, Evelyn, you'll be out here jumping over broomsticks when I'm dead and gone.' He was good at heart but hateful.

"I just barely remember the hospital down there because I was little. Dr. Tidmarsh was the one that was our doctor. I was scared to death of him. When I went by there, I would run like crazy cause I was afraid he was gonna catch me and put me in there. Now that's how I felt about hospitals when I was little and I never did go in one. I thought they just reached out, grabbed you and put you in there. Well, they wasn't gonna snatch me up... I got gone! Dr. Tidmarsh had a good little hospital and he was there a long time. In Whittier we had our own doctor for a long time.

"That's the way it was when I was a child. There were no specialty stores, only big stores that had everything. People came in on the train, and if they had to wait a night, they stayed at the Parton Hotel till they could catch another train. Whittier was the place to catch a train or to go do anything."

One day I asked Evelyn to give me a tour of Whittier. We got into her car, and off we went. She drove as I held a pad and piece of paper for note taking. As we rode through the tiny village the memories rolled. She showed me the old Revis Store where Sam Queen called the square dances on Saturday night. On the corner the post office now stands, where once was the gas station she and her husband ran for years.

The McHan Hotel still stands on the corner but looks lonely as it no longer receives guests. Evelyn showed me where the house once stood in which she grew up. We rode along, her talking and me busily making notes. I plotted out the town on the little map that I brought.

Evelyn often spoke of wanting to see the little village of Whittier as it once was back then. It's heyday is long gone but small town charm is still alive and well in Whittier. Today it's much smaller but still is a beautiful place to visit and enjoy. There are a few businesses located there today: Stuff and Such, Oxford Hardware, Whittier Mattress Sales, and Parton's Law Office are all thriving businesses. In Whittier folks still

The Original Whittier Hotel   1890's

tains are a dime a dozen. People are racing to the mountains, moving into homes where trees and pasture once stood. It may come as a surprise, but the situation was similar in Junaluska in 1881. Dr. Clark Whittier, a native of Canada, arrived in Junaluska in 1881 and purchased 60,000 acres of mountain land. He divided the land into lots and sold it to settlers. He also had plans for a summer resort that was never

help one another, aren't in much of a hurry, and they always say "Hello" when they pass.

Today, developers cutting up the hills and moun-

about to prosper, as its location placed it grand central for rail and timber access.

Clark Whittier was a wealthy developer, but he was not a developer in the cut and run style of the 21st century. The new town was his town, and he played a vital part in its development. He helped build several buildings in built, atop Clingman's Dome.

Whittier had a vision of the future. He recognized the value of the virgin timber in the area, and saw the coming of the railroad. It was being built west from Salisbury to connect with the copper mines in Copper Hill, Tennessee. Until his arrival, the area was known as Junaluska. The town of Whittier was now

---

PART III, PATRIOTIC.

Quartette: "The News Boys."
Song: "Battle Hymn of the Republic."
Recitations: A tribute to President McKinley,
....................ALGERIA STEVENS.
The Martial Spirit, ... GLEN MILLER.
Bingen on the Rhine, ... SALLIE PARKS.
Oration: Causes of the Spanish-American
War.............GILMORE WELCH.
Recitations: Death in a Spanish Prison, ETHEL TERRELL,
Our Flying Squadron, ...MARIA WRIGHT.
One More Volunteer,.....GARLAND JONES
The Volunteer on the Shelf, LILLY MILLER.
Dialogue: BORROWING NEIGHBORS, { MEEK KERLEE,
{ ADDIE GIBBS.
Song: "Tenting on the Old Camp Ground."
Recitations: The White Rose,.........EMMA MCHAN.
An Incident of the Civil War, ROSE ZACHARY,
The "Glory" of War, ...EDNA HAYES.
Yankee Fitz Lee, ... VINNIE STEVENS.
Song: "Dixie."
Drill: The Whittier Cadets.
Song: "Farewell."

EXHIBITION

OF THE

WHITTIER HIGH SCHOOL,

Whittier, N. C.,   May 27, 1898.

————0————

——PROGRAM OUTLINE——

Morning Session, 9 o'clock,
Oral Examination of Classes.

Afternoon Session, 2 o'clock,
Exercises by the Primary Department,
Followed by an Address
By Hon. James H. Cathey

| | AFTERNOON SESSION: | |

Song: "Happy School Days Now are Passing."
Recitations: Vacation Time, ...NANCY THOMPSON.
Papa's Letter,..........VELMA SHAW.
God Sees, ...NELLIE KING.
A Little School Ma'm,...LIZZIE ZACHARY.
The Silver Lining,....CARRIE THOMPSON.
Song: "A Home by the Sea."
Recitations: God's Work, ...MARIAH THOMAS.
The School,...........NORA MASSEY.
The Little Speaker,......TROY MCLEAN.
The Grumbler, ...BESSIE HOLWORTH.
A Dream,............DICK KERLEE.
B Lesson for Tommy,...FRED TEAGUE,
Song: "The Working Boy."
Dialogue: Not Quite a Bargain ...... { MINNIE ZACHARY
{ VINNIE MCLEAN.
Recitations: Harry's Mistake,...........DICK KING
Adam Never Was a Boy, CHARLIE TEAGUE.
The Witch Child,.... MAMIE MILLR.
Vacation Song,..........LOVE THOMAS.
The Sweetest Little Girl,. JESSIE BIGHAM.
Three Little Mothers.
Song: "I'll Try."
Recitations: In the Kitchen, ... MYRTLE BIGHAM.
The Old Man Wants to Fight, C. WILSON.
Doll Drill.
Recitation: Farewell, Friends, ...VINNIE MCLEAN.
Address, by .....HON. JAS. H. CATHEY.
Song: "Vacation"

| | EVENING SESSION: | |

Song: "Good Evening."
Invocation, followed by Chant of Lord's Prayer.
Statement Concerning the School.

PART I. EDUCATIONAL.

Essays: Discipline in the Free School, HATTIE ZACHARY.
Suggestions in Reference to Reading, ROXIE TABOR.
Some Difficulties in Free School
Teaching,..............ADDIE GIBBS.
Who Should Teach in the Free
School? ....LAURA MCHAN.
Debate: Should Western North Carolina
Have a Compulsory School Law?
Affirmative, JOHN WELCH.
Negative, WALTER WILSON.

PART II, MISCELLANEOUS.

Song: "The Hunter's Chorus."

THE LILY MARCH.

Recitation: The Boys We Want,........ ORA JONES.
Accountability, ...JENNIE STEVENS.
Essay: The New South,............FLORA BATTLE.
Recitation: The "Pahty,".........GRACE KERLEE.
Song: "A Letter from Home."
Play: THE SNIGGLES FAMILY.

My Mountain Granny

Whittier, and was the first owner of Whittier Lumber Company, a large saw mill that was operated by several people until the 1930's. On June 29, 1886, he deeded a plot of land for the Whittier Methodist Episcopal Church.

He didn't cut and run, because it was easier to build a town, than to pack his belongings and leave. Had he done so, he would have ridden east, by buggy or mule, to the nearest access point for the railroad. The trip would have taken days, if he had gone in the summer. In the Winter, there would have been no trip.

At the time of his arrival, the area was wilderness.

It was a land of opportunity; wild game roamed the area and virgin timber covered the area. Land could be purchased for five cents per acre. Roads consisted of rutted trails, wide enough for a wagon in some places, and others for a horse. In the Winter, they were so muddy and marred up that nothing moved. The saying, "Lord Willing and the Creek Don't Rise," held a lot of meaning in the old days.

Bridges didn't exist, and Whittier had several fords where the water was low and safe to cross. A wooden bridge was first constructed in Whittier in 1907. Foot bridge's were an old log laid across creek and they

Early Whittier

Whittier

were very common. There were no dams back then for flood control. Often the creek or the river left it's banks, stranding people until it receded.

There were no hospitals and few businesses. The few brave people who lived in the area lived by their wits. They were their own blacksmith, doctor, seamstress, veterinarian, carpenter, and farmer. The local family didn't deal in currency. They bartered and traded for what they couldn't make themselves. It was a land of make-do or do-without.

The railroad was coming, and Clark Whittier saw its changing power. It brought the first light of civilization to an area that was landlocked and isolated from the rest of the world. The railroad was the forerunner of today's interstate system. It arrived in Whittier in 1884, and the first passenger ticket was sold for passage to Clyde by railroad agent E.M. Scruggs. Standard fare at the time was two-and-a-half cent per mile.

With the railroad now having arrived, Dr. Whittier called a public meeting for the purpose of establishing a town. The meeting was held at the junction of Conley's Creek and the Tuckaseegee River on August 19, 1885. Dr. Whittier was the center of attention. He opened the meeting by saying " I move that we start operations here upon the word of God, including morality and especially temperance and prohibition of the strongest form."

Prayer was given by a man named W.H. Cooper. He prayed that Whittier, "Be free from epidemic and noisome politicians, that it's widows never be turned away empty, and that the wayfaring man find lodging there."

Later, a petition was given for road construction projects. A grade road to Leatherman Gap and the Macon County line was proposed. The road would be later known as Conley's Creek.

Prospectors and land speculators were common, but none like Dr. Whittier. He owned 60,000 acres, and anyone coming to the area to settle, dealt with Clark Whittier. Considering the large amount of property he owned and the enormous growth around the corner , Clark Whittier was in position to become very wealthy.

It was not to be, for he had been in failing health for some time and died on May 27, 1887, just a couple of years after his town was founded. At his request, he was buried on a hill above the town.

My Mountain Granny

The railroad gave Whittier's residents jobs, brought in goods they couldn't raise or make, took them places, carried visitors to them, and provided excitement. The train whistle provided a way of telling time, because it was always prompt. Prior to the railroads, arrival mail was delivered on horseback from Sevierville, Tennessee. The obstacles of this type of delivery were staggering. Critical news of a loved ones sickness or death could arrive days later.

In the early 1900's four passenger trains arrived daily. Two arrived from Murphy at 10:00 a.m. and 3 p.m. The other two came from Asheville at 12:00 pm and 7:00 pm. James Eric Whishunt was the agent and telegrapher from 1912-1920. Folks could send and receive telegrams at the depot through Western Union.

Soon after the railroad's arrival, three side rails were constructed to serve several lumber mills nearby. One, in particular, was a large lumber mill located in the Revis Bottom, and operated in the 30's by Scott

Whittier

Ashe. They capitalized on the virgin timber in the area, cutting it into lumber and shipping it out by rail. Most of the lumber mills were smaller, but there were several larger ones. Champion Paper had a huge band mill at Ravensford. Loggers were paid fifteen to twenty dollars per thousand board-feet of lumber, a nice paycheck in a day when bartering was common and cash was scarce.

The railroad and timber industry required a large workforce, and the majority of Whittier families depended on them for their living. It also helped other industries, particularly farming. Many people shipped cattle to market by train.

Before the railroad, they had to drive them on foot to market. The train also brought in livestock and goods needed for farming.

Shortly after the railroad came, a depot was constructed. There was a holding pen behind it, and cattle

Steam engine for the Whittier Saw Mill located at the north end of town.   c. late 1890's

My Mountain Granny

and other livestock were raised for shipment to major markets such as Atlanta. They were put in the holding pen, and then into a leading chute to load them into the cattle cars.

The depot was a center of community life. Every kind of goods that a family could use such as lamps, tables, chairs and beds came through the town depot. It was more than just merchandise though because the depot and the railroad meant something to people. Folks met family that had come for a visit. Evelyn Beck recalled taking a trip to Asheville with her dad and sister and arriving back late that night. People remembered the first time they saw the train as youngsters and heard its whistle. Some who had no fare to ride caught a free ride by hiding in a freight car or running alongside and jumping on.

There were two hotels in Whittier. The Teague House was built about the same time as the Whittier hotel. It was run by Mattie Teague Parton and Silas L. Teague. It had a livery stable and when needed served as a hospital. Alexander Hamilton Hayes and his wife Margarete built the Whittier hotel around the turn of the century. It became known as the McHan Hotel.

The McHan Hotel was ran by Eva Summerow

McHan and Robert McHan. Robert McHan was from a family of educators. All of his brothers and sisters received their teacher training at Cullowhee.

The biggest school in Swain County at the time was in Ravensford, where Robert McHan taught school. Later Mchan moved his family to Whittier and taught school a couple of years there before suffering a stroke, and becoming an invalid for seven years before his death at the age of fifty-two.

The McHan family first ran the Parton Hotel across from the depot before buying the McHan Hotel. I spoke with Wilma Ashe a couple of years back. She had fond memories of her mother, Eva, and the hotel.

"We were living in Whittier during the Depression and if it hadn't been for my mama being a wise person and working so hard at the hotel, we'd never have made it. She fed us and kept us alive," she told me.

McHan Hotel catered to large numbers of people including the drummers coming through. They would come into town, rent a room at one of the hotels, and a horse and buggy from the livery stable. They would travel around peddling apple trees, grapevines, sewing machines or anything they could sell. They would take the orders, then send the merchandise back on the

40

Whittier

train. Colonel Raymond Robbins also stayed at McHan Hotel while on escape from Washington in 1932.

The hotel had fourteen rooms and cost one dollar a night, including meals. The mass exodus that occurred in the 30's and 40's took away much of the hotel's business. After the hotel closed, the front portion of it was used as a barber shop by Ike Parris until the mid 1980's. The hotel still stands and is privately owned. It is well over 100 years old, making it one of the only original Whittier businesses still standing.

The most infamous to have ever walked through the doors of the Whittier hotel, was James Lattimore Himrod. He arrived in Whittier in 1910, and claimed he was

the Corresponding Secretary of the Industrial Education league of the South. He promoted a new school called the Whittier Collegiate and Agricultural Institute. Himrod promoted the new school as providing students an industrial education that would prepare them for the future. The local people were of a progressive nature. They

Three miles from Whittier, on Battle Cove Knob, was a large dead oak tree that was used by Col. Raymond Robbins as a lookout while he was living in Whittier under the name of Reynold H. Rogers. At the base, pine needles made a soft carpet. Within a hole in the tree was found a large piece of waterproof paper which Col. Robbins kept there and wore when it rained. Fat pine knots for use in starting a fire also were found in the tree opening. Near the tree was a crude wooden altar surmounted by a cross made by Col. Robbins.

wanted better schools to teach their children and widely embraced Himrod's idea. The school was planned to be built on land owned by Dr. Teague and was to cover sixty-five acres. The school was to be a modern facility with spacious rooms and indoor plumbing. It would consist of dormitories, fire escapes and all modern improvements. It was proposed that there would be an orchard on the grounds.

Himrod also had a plan for providing meals the first year. Since the school year wouldn't start until September 1st, the school would require at least one thousand gallons of canned fruit. He encouraged the prospective students to make provisions for the school. Anything would be accepted, including string beans, sauerkraut, dried apples, dried corn, potatoes, dried beans, beets, turnips, and cabbage.

The school would then purchase these items at fair market value and help the students pay their tuition. Work was to begin immediately, and the school was to open by September 1st. Whittier was excited that Himrod was carrying on the dreams of Dr. Whittier, who desired his town to grow and prosper.

Himrod also started Whittier's only newspaper,

1913
Himrod Day
Celebration

The Whittier Record. It cost one dollar per year, but its only issue was printed on May 30, 1913. Soon after its debut, it was found that James Lattimore Himrod was a shyster and the Whittier Collegiate and

A BIG BOOST

Monster Mass Meeting

Court House Waynesville

Thursday Evening, May 22, 8 O'clock

A Meeting in the interest of the Whittier Collegiate and Agricultural Institute.

SPEAKERS

James Lattimore Himrod.
President W. C. and A. Institute

J. Ulrich Gibbs - Secretary Board of Trustees

Alexander H. Hayes
Member Swain County Board of Education

Come and hear these speakers they are live ones.

"Mr. Himrod is an earnest, forceful, and impressive speaker. He holds his audience from the beginning."

J. Ulrich Gibbs

WHITTIER RECORD   May 30, 191

R. J. ROANE & CO.

Whittier. N. C.

Headquarters for all classes of Merchandise. We make the right prices.

Come to us for your Dry Goods, Hats, Shirts, Clothing, Pants, underwear and Gloves.

We have the largest stock of shoes in this teritory. Our Hardware line is more complete than ever. See our stoves, Ranges, Turning Plows, Harrows, Cultivators, Mowers, Rakes and wagons. We have a complete line of New Furniture, Sewing Machines, Trunks and Matting.

We are agents for The International Harvester Company's farm Machinery

"The Best Goods at the Lowest Prices"

Whittier Drug Co.

A full line of Drugs and Staple articles.

GIVE OUR SODA FOUNTAIN A TRAL THESE HOT DAYS.

Whittier - - N. C.

WHITTIER RECORD   PAGE THR

A. H. AND M. E. HAYES AND COMPANY

Staple and Fancy Dry Goods, Underwear, Hosery, Gloves, Neckwear, Men's Furnishings, Small wears and Fancy Goods, Ladie's Suits and Dresses, Men's and Boys' Suits, Shoes and Hats for Everybody.

Our merchandise offers large inducements, for certainly a number of valued customers, new and old, have shown substantial approval.

Let us have the pleasure of serving you please

We'll try to merit your approval

GEORGE T. REDMOND

BARBER

Don't go elsewhere to get Shaved, come here

Whittier - - N. C.

Ads taken from Whittier's only newspaper, The Whittier Record. It was to cost $1.00 per year, but its only issue was printed on May 30, 1913.

My Mountain Granny

Agricultural Institute a hoax. Lattimore had skipped town with Whittier's dreams, and hard-earned dollars in his satchel.

A buggy, or hack as it was called, was the main form of transportation at the time, and Whittier had several blacksmith shops through the years. They did a good business repairing buggies and shoeing horses.

William Turner Lewis ran a blacksmith shop in Whittier for years. He did blacksmith work, made caskets, pulled teeth and was a jack-of-all-trades.

One day he was shoeing a horse with his helper Henry Vinegum. A feller walked up to him and poked the horse he was shoeing in the side with a stick. The horse kicked Mr. Lewis near across the road. Grandpa Lewis hollered, "What in the Hell did you do that for?"

The man then said, "Because I wanted to." As the man turned to walk away, Grandpa Lewis grabbed a branding iron and placed it on his rearend. The man let out a scream that could be heard for miles and sat down in some water nearby.

The man hollered, "What did you do that for?"

"Because I wanted to," Grandpa Lewis replied.

The man was "hot," and he hopped up ready to

fight. Grandpa banished a knife and sliced him.

Henry Vinegum said, "Grandpa, ain't no way a man bleeding like that's gonna live."

The man lived because it wasn't blood that Henry was seeing—Grandpa had sliced the man right down to his bright red underwear.

The calaboose was located above Roane and Varner's Store next to the tracks. It served as a voting place, but primarily as a jail for town rowdies and drunks. It was a plank jail. Its one holding room was rigged with planks that held the drunks till they sobered up. There was never any serious crime, only the occasional rowdy drunk or a fistfight every so often.

Whittier

Down through the years, Whittier's residents have gotten along pretty well, and have taken care of one another as best they could. Whittier incorporated in 1885, and there have only been two murders within the town limits. Carl Elliott was murdered by Jim Griffin in 1932, in front of Revis Store. In 1960, Jewel Davis killed Lester Green in the old Ferguson Store.

From the town's incorporation, prohibition and temperance of the strongest form were enforced. In the 1890, the order of the "Sons of Temperance," gave a public performance of songs and speeches speaking against Demon Rum. It's likely that this was a positive influence on those in attendance.

As for those that didn't make it to the performance, they continued on as usual. Apparently prohibition in the town limits only applied to saloons and drinking establishments. Saloons were outlawed, but it was not illegal for groups of citizens to order whiskey in barrels which they could serve to the public who gathered around them.

Demon rum kept the calaboose in business. One night, Davey Wadesutt and James Owl were locked up for public drunkenness. It was a cold winter night, and they built a fire in the middle of the floor, which, of course, set the whole building on fire.

One night when Dr. Bennett was mayor of Whittier, a man attempted to operate a saloon without a permit. He opened his saloon with a bulldog pistol pointed in the face of the mayor and the marshal. Mayor Bennett instructed the marshal to

Old window from the Whittier prison.

ANUARY 9,1890

LETTER FROM WHITTIER

Dear Herald--Whittier is looking forward ith much interest to the coming spring hen it is rumored that there will be a ransfer of the Whittier estate and a yndicate of northern capitalists will esume the Whittier enterprise.

Last Friday night the order of the Sons f Temperance of this place gave a public ntertainment that was donducted in the ollowing style. Rev. J.H.Jenkins opened he exercises with on of his stirring prayers. Then came vocal music and as the last notes were wafted away in the night air, Miss C.A.McConnell arose and read an essay, "A Drunkards Dream." Rev. A.M.West then delivered a temperande lecture. An essay was read by Miss Minnie Bryson, subject, "Hang out the Temperance Banner." Then came the orater of the occassion, Rev. P.P.McLean. The humorous way in which this gentleman delivered his remarks was both amusing and impressive. As the speaker closed, calls were made for Charlie Massie who appeared on the platform and delivered a short and pointed address, giving his experience with King Alcohol, the many strugles he had had with this demon of strong drink. Miss Mary Wright read an essay on "Lips That Touch Liquor Shall Never Touch Mine." with such spirit as to convince the audience that she was in earnest. the closing speech and S.W.Cooper delivered the closing speech by Rev.J.H.Jenkin the audience was dismissed by Rev.J.H.Jenkin
                                    More Anon.
                                    You Know Who

JANUARY 30, 1890

Rev. P.P.McLean was in town Monday. Dr. Scruggs went to Whittier Tuesday. S.W.Cooper was down from Whittier one day last week

45

arrest the saloon keeper and throw him in the cala-boose. The man fought, but only until Dr Bennett had broken his best Winchester hunting rifle over his head.

Whittier was fortunate to have several doctors at its service over the years. Dr. A.M. Bennett, also its first mayor, served for several years. When Dr. Bennett left, James Teague served for several years.

The most well-known and the doctor most longtime residents remember was Dr. Harold Tidmarsh from Whitmire, South Carolina. His office was located across from the depot. He served hero-ically during the flu epidemic of 1918-1919, traveling many miles on horseback to visit the sick. He kept wire cutters in his bag, and would cut the fence across the pasture if it meant saving distance and time in reaching his patient.

In the early 1900's, the fee for delivering a baby was $10.00. Often families didn't have money to pay, and the doctor would be paid with potatoes or whatev-er the family could spare to give him. Once a local doctor was called upon to deliver a baby. It was Winter and he traveled miles through the mud and the cold to the mother's side. After the baby was born,

Dr. Harold Tidmarsh's office

he gave the dad the bill. The man looked at him puz-zled and said, "Sorry, Doctor, I ain't got it!"

The doctor rolled his eyes and said, "You've known about this for nine months! I've traveled ten miles and delivered you a healthy baby! This is what you owe." The doctor rode away with a sack of pota-toes at his side.

Roan and Varner's Store was run by R.J. Roane and Cerbern Varner. It was the biggest store between Asheville and Murphy and supplied everything a mountain family needed. They sold old-timey washing machines, caskets, wagons, clothes and food. They had huge barrels of vinegar that they would pump into the jug that you brought. They also had cured meats that they would slice and sell according to the customer's needs. In the 30's, a 24 lb sack of flour cost $1.20, coffee 8 cents per pound, and eggs 4 cents a dozen.

The store was positioned right next to the railroad, and its business depended heavily upon it. Much of the lumbering in the area was made into crossties for the railroad. People would sell the crossties to Roane and Varner and be paid in Doogaloo money. Roane and Varner would in turn sell them to Southern Railways.

Folks would bring items of all sorts to Roane and Varner's to sell and would be paid in Doogaloo money. This was Roane and Varner's own currency with their name printed boldly on the front. It was made of aluminum and came in 5, 10, 25, and 50 cent pieces. Doogaloos could only be spend on goods at Roane and Varner's Store.

The store had credit extended far and wide to Murphy and all points in between. When the Depression hit, it dealt a heavy blow. Mountain families were in need of everything. These people had been loyal customers of Roane and Varner's, and naturally the store extended credit to them, knowing much of the money would never be repaid.

At one point Roane and Varner had purchased a large number of crossties which the railroad refused to buy, claiming that they were defective. The railroad also stopped buying crossties after railroad work had moved West. These factors contributed to the store's filing bankruptcy in 1937 and closing i's doors forever.

Revis Hardware was founded in 1926 by John Revis. At the time, the only equipment he had to dig out the bank with was a mule, pan scrape, pick and shovel. It took him a year just to move the dirt. He scattered the fill dirt, to the site where the old Shell station was located and all about Whittier.

People all over town were talking about John Revis. They said he was crazy for starting a business there. In

A copy of a newspaper clipping:

Homes Without Capital 1886
THE FOUNDING OF THE TOWN OF **WHITTIER**
SOMETHING UNIQUE AND NEW

Clark Whittier of California is dividing 60,000 Acres of land in Swain Co N.C., in the Skyland Region into small tracts for actual settlers only. They will be sold for cash or on a credit of one to ten years. If desirable the principle may lay for five years at 6 percent. Interest payable annually and one - fifth of the principle to be paid each year thereafter.

The soil is rich, its tobacco brings the highest price in the market, averaging a net profit of from 75 to 150 dollars per acre. 250 acres of land are being cleared to rent on shares for tobacco growers. The lands are divided into farms from 20 to 100 acres to suit purchasers.

The labor required in opening these lands has made the town of Whittier a necessity which is now a station on the Western North Carolina Railroad, 6 miles east of Charleston. The founder of Whittier will spare no pains or expense to make it the most attractive and desirable resident and business town in Western North Carolina.

Mills stores, residences and a fine hotel are now being erected and other manufactories will follow. Lots are being donated to churches, schools, public buildings and works.The improvements of the lands and the town requires all kinds of mechanics and laborers and all purchasers of lands and lots can get immediate and constant employment at common labor. Purchasers will be furnished lumber for improvements at $10 to 12$ per 1000 feet and work to pay for it.

Comfortable quarters and rations will be provided for purchasers and their family at the acre cost of rations until they can erect their homes. Come right along. Thus you can buy lands, lots and build homes, on long credits and work to pay for them.

Such inducements have never been offered before as they are now offered in Whittier. Come at once and erect your houses. Plenty of work at fair prices. Tobacco lands to clear and ready for the spring crops. Fences are being erected. Come and buy land soon.

C. Whittier • Whittier, Charleston P. O. • Swain Co. N.C.

Whittier

1926, there was no main road through Whittier, and most of the businesses were in Swain County on the opposite side of town.

Roane and Varner was the biggest store between Asheville and Murphy and people said they had business sewed up in Whittier. Folks were counting the days until Revis Store folded. It didn't fold, and it prospered for 8o years. Soon after it was built, a main road came through town and businesses began shifting to Jackson County, the side of town where his store was located.

Perhaps the reason it lasted through hard times was that John Revis had lots of irons in the fire. In the 30's, half of the property was leased out for a car dealership. At one time, a restaurant operated out of it, and later on, he began selling hardware and dry goods. The upstairs portion of the building was used partially for living quarters and the other part for a dance hall.

John lived upstairs, and at the time, the only phone in Whittier was located downstairs in his store. John would wake up at all hours of the night and walk downstairs to let folks who had an emergency or who needed to call a doctor, use the telephone.

The square dances that John Revis held upstairs were a huge event. People would come from miles around, and the town would be filled with wagons and buggies, for the big event at Revis Store. Sam Queen would come all the way from Waynesville to call the square dance. He'd bring his band with him, and the square dance would go on until the wee hours of the morning.

When Fontana Lake was built, it flooded the old communities of Japan, Judson, Hazel Creek, Bushnel and Proctor. John Revis bought up some of the old homes. He rebuilt them in and around Whittier, selling and renting some. Rent at the time was $10 or $15 dollars a month, a hefty sum in hard-scrabble times.

John Revis was a good man who was good to people. He sold a lot on credit during the Depression . Folks would come in the store needing a bag of flour or sugar, and he would put it on credit. He knew full well they would pay him back if they could, but it was the Hoover days, and times were so hard it was likely he wouldn't see the money again. The old saying, "What goes around comes around," is the honest truth. John Revis's generosity in hard times was a

My Mountain Granny

good deed by a good man, but it built his reputation and brought him business when times got better.

Until the 1920's, there were no stock laws in the mountains. A mountain family could keep a large number of hogs, more than the land they owned could support. They would go to the courthouse and get their own earmark, brand their animals and turn them out into the woods. Chestnuts were plentiful at that time, and the hogs would fatten up on them and be ready for slaughter in the Fall. This method required little effort from the farmer, except for rounding them up in the Fall. When stock laws were passed in the 30's, farmers could no longer keep the livestock they had.

In the old days, Whittier echoed with the sound of the train whistle and the shriek of the sawmill. Whittier boomed because the railroad and logging industry thrived. As long as they were strong, Whittier hummed along as usual. In the mid 20's Whittier was booming, its streets packed on Saturdays with buggies. Folks socialized and got the news from each other. They traded and enjoyed each

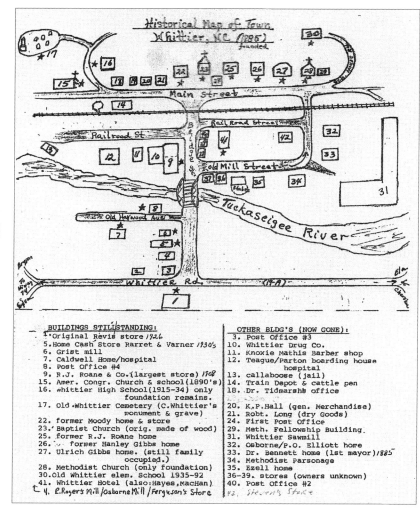

BUILDINGS STILL STANDING:
4. Original Revis store 1926
5. Home Cash Store Rarret & Varner 1930's
6. Grist mill
7. Caldwell Home/hospital
8. Post Office #4
9. R.J. Roane & Co. (largest store) 1908
15. Amer. Congr. Church & school (1890's)
16. Whittier High School (1915-34) only foundation remains.
17. Old Whittier Cemetery (C.Whittier's monument & grave)
22. former Moody home & store
23. Baptist Church (orig. made of wood)
25. former R.J. Roane home
26. former Hanley Gibbs home
27. Ulrich Gibbs home. (still family occupied.)
28. Methodist Church (only foundation)
30. Old Whittier elem. School 1935-92
41. Whittier Hotel (also:Hayes,MacHan).
4. R.Rogers Mill/Osborne Mill/Ferguson's Store

OTHER BLDG'S (NOW GONE):
3. Post Office #3
10. Whittier Drug Co.
11. Knoxie Mathis Barber shop
12. Teague/Parton boarding house hospital
13. callaboose (jail)
14. Train Depot & cattle pen
18. Dr. Tidmarsh office
20. K.P.Hall (gen. Merchandise)
21. Robt. Long (dry Goods)
24. First Post Office
29. Meth. Fellowship Building.
31. Whittier Sawmill
32. Osborne/P.O. Elliott home
33. Dr. Bennett home (1st mayor)/1885
34. Methodist Parsonage
35. Ezell home
36-39. stores (owners unknown)
40. Post Office #2
42. Stevens Store

other's company. Whittier was at its zenith, and it was ahead of its time. It provided all the services of a modern city. It had two hotels, a livery stable, a

50

railroad, a jail, mayor, sheriff, doctor, and depot. At one time, it even had a photographic studio ran by J. Robert Childers.

Whittier's weakness was that its economy wasn't diversified. It was founded on the lumber industry, and timber was it's lifeblood for the next fifty years. The Stock Market crashed in 1929 and signaled the beginning of the Great Depression. Everything grinded to a halt, including the timber industry. With this, the railroad began laying off people. Evelyn Beck's father, Harley Howell, made it until 1935 until the railroad laid him off.

This left Whittier's residents in a predicament. Local families had lived in the area for years, some since The Trail of Tears, and they didn't cotton to packing and leaving. Gradually they left, many for the cotton mills around Gastonia and Belmont. Later on people began moving to Washington State for jobs in the timber industry. World War II came along on the hills of the Depression, and the economy picked up, but by then, many local families had moved. In 1940, the National Park was created and large stands of timber around Ravensford and Smokemont would never hear the hum of the sawmill again. This spelled the end of the timber boom.

Our country is now mired in a recession, and we often hear that hard times are upon us. People are worried about another Depression, and I recently visited with Bill Lewis and discussed hard times with him. He said, " The poorest man in the U.S. lives like a king compared to the way we lived. Modern-day America doesn't have the stamina or the skills to survive hard times as our ancestors did. Today's generation reminisces about the 'Good Old Days.' The modern generation lives a pampered life. We get excited when, Heaven forbid, the power goes out for several hours or when we have to call the repairman for our cable service. I have a hunch that, if we were to have our wish granted and found ourself in the year 1925, we would be in for a rude awakening. We'd light the cook stove and cook on it a time or so, haul water from the spring for our weekly bath, and trot out to the outhouse on a Winter day and proclaim, 'I've had it! Send me back to the good old days!'

We can't relive the past, but we can learn from it. Whittier was fortunate to have some good and decent folks living in its town. I've only met a few, but I wish I could sit and talk with all of them. They worked

My Mountain Granny

hard, not wanting for anything except what was earned with their own two hands. They were God-fearing people who lived by the Good Book and were committed to their churches. The older generation were fighters. They lived through hardships that the modern generation can't imagine: the hard times of the Depression, the Flood, and the War. The people of Whittier took care of each other. In the condition today's society is in, those are principles we can hang our hat on today, tomorrow, and forever.

During the 1930's, entertainment was of the make-your-own variety. Radio was in its infancy, TV was nonexistent, and few people had telephones. If you wanted entertainment, you made your own fun.

The hardships that Whittier's residents have encountered over the years have been well-documented here in "My Mountain Granny," but there was a lighter side to the life they lived. I doubt that if you were to go back to 1930 and walk down Whittier's main street, you'd not see many people hanging their heads. They soldiered on, making the best of difficult circumstances, and whenever possible, they had a grand old time.

An Old Camp Meeting

People had corn-shuckings, bean-stringings and square dances. Churches were a center of social life, but two big events in the fall of the year were camp meetings and medicine shows.

Today, when you ride through Whittier, the post office sits on the corner across from the old Revis Store. The lot has held several different businesses over the years, including the Shell station that Evelyn and Julius ran for several years after

My Mountain Granny

WWII, but in the old days it was the site of several events providing a grand old time for Whittier's residents.

In the old days after a crop was "laid by," camp meetings were held at this location. They usually started the first Saturday and Sunday of August after a crop was gathered, and people were at leisure. The fun lasted four to six weeks or until fodder-pulling time. Because travel was rough and people came from miles around, they stayed and camped out on site or stayed at a home nearby with family or friends.

People brought fresh vegetables from their gardens and fresh meat from the farm.

The event was full of religious fervor. The local churches would come together in revival. The days events would be held under an old tent or an arbor and would often alternate between singing and preaching. Often local singers would sing old hymns. One such quartet that Bill Lewis remembered was Old Man Hardy Crisp, George Chastain and Nancy and Ben Bushyhead.

Singing and preaching would last and build up to the point of the altar call. This was also called the misery seat, as seekers would go forward. The call went on sometimes for hours, while shouting and singing continued. The seekers moved between "the light" and "the darkness." As the camp meeting came to a close, there was a special baptizing for those who had seen "the light."

MEDICINE SHOWS

The medicine show was the model for commercial radio and television—free entertainment interspersed with sales pitches.

The shows were structured around entertainers who could be expected to draw a crowd who would listen to, and then, undoubtedly purchase the medicines offered by the "doctor" who made two or three sales pitches a night. Medicine

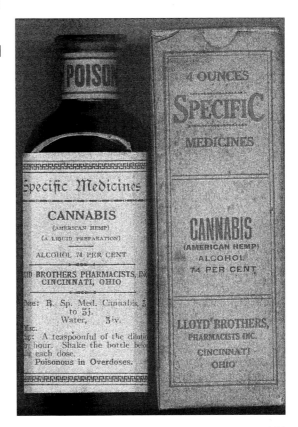

The medicine show was held on the corner in Whittier. It would be held for a whole week and would bring people from far and wide. It is now an event that exists only in the history books.

Medicine shows could be deemed health-oriented entertainment traveling by horse and buggy and sponsored by the major medicine companies. These teams peddled miracle medications and other products between various entertainment acts. These were the days before TV, so the medicine show could be considered the beginning of today's info-mercial.

shows were a combination of singing, fiddling, square dancing, story telling or juggling, mixed with with pitches for medicines that were supposed to cure anything from stomach to warts or the common cold.

Whittier possessed plenty of local entertainment. They would have fiddling contests during the show sponsored by some of the local businesses, who provided a nice prize.

One year the one and only Bill Monroe came to Whittier and sang as part of the medicine show.

Medicine show entertainers had to be astonishingly versatile. Shows depended heavily on repeat business during their stay in a community. To get it, they were often forced to change their bills every night for a run of one or two weeks. At least one company produced a substantially new show every night for forty nights in a row. Since medicine show performers usually appeared two or three times a night and sometimes more, the size of a performer's repertoire had to be enormous.

The product most commonly associated with medicine shows was an elixir, commonly known as snake oil. It was touted to cure diseases, smooth facial wrinkles, remove stains in clothing, prolong life, or cure any number of common ailments. In late nineteenth century America, physicians were scarce and poorly educated. Treatments might include such things as bleeding using live leeches, cold baths, blistering agents, and other remedies that often were worse than the ail-

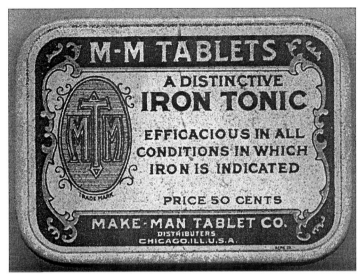

ments that they were meant to treat.

Many people placed their faith in patent medicines, pitched by traveling salesmen who never failed to entertain the crowds before offering cure-alls. Modern advertising was born during this era, as patent medicine companies printed almanacs with useful information and humorous quotations, mixed with plenty of advertising for mail-order herbal remedies. The newspapers and magazines of the day were crammed with ads for medicines and miracle-cure devices. Most of these medicines were, at best, harmless; many contained generous quantities of alcohol, opium or cocaine, ensuring a quick feeling of well-being for first-time customers.

The medicines of the day may have been nicknamed "snake oil," but it was all there was available before the days of modern medicine. They may not have cured anything, but with generous doses of alcohol or opium they made people feel like a million dollars if they didn't kill them first.

57

Chapter 9

THE SHOW CAN'T GO ON

mainly were responsibility of the artists, who wore the hats of manager, singer, accountant and bouncer. Artists had to be tough and not afraid of a knock.

Country singers such as Minnie Pearl, String bean, and Grandpappy, mostly played small venues

The Carter Family and Jimmie Rodgers were pioneers in the 1920's and led country music from the front porch to the front stage. In the 1950s country music walked the line between oral tradition and its growth towards the opportunity to purchase records and listen to it on the radio primarily through the Grand Old Opry.

Country Music wasn't big business, not in comparison to the mega stars of today. There were no videos, or stadium tours and the life wasn't luxurious. Acts didn't have the big entourage of today. Many performers traveled in small package tours or as single acts. Tour buses were a thing of the future, most artists crammed into the back of a old car such as a Cadillac, equipment and all. Security and tour managers were twenty years into the future. These duties

such as the fair or a schoolhouse. The stage at the old Whittier school saw the likes of these stars. Bill Monroe and Hank Williams were the closet things to stars in that day. Bill made to Whittier; Hank was scheduled but didn't make it.

Many performers of the day had a byline such as "Honey, hush!" For a week or so after the show someone would holler across the street, "Honey, hush!" The person would understand the good word and pass it on.

Whittier was typical of the small time markets that acts played in that day. Various country singers performed in Whittier and some never forgot the small town. The singers were of course accessible, they might have been seen in Revis Store or at McHan Hotel in a break between shows. There wasn't often the need for security but from time to time it would have come in handy.

One night Grand Old Opry star Grandpappy was giving a couple of shows on the small wooden stage at the Old Whittier school. In between perform- ances he did a little comedy. He gave a clever grin that indicated something was about to happen.

Grandpappy chuckled, "Now I've kissed every pretty girl in this room. If there's one that I haven't smooched raise your hand and I'll give you a big one right now!" He noticed Theodore Lewis sitting proud in the third row with his girlfriend Florence Chastain. Grandpappy pointed at Florence and "Yelled I ain't kissed her pretty lips yet!" He jumped off the stage, walked up to Florence and gave her a big kiss. Theodore turned as red as a ripe tomato. He socked Grandpappy right in the jaw. The lights went out on Grandpappy and the show was over. Gene Reid was a witness to the spectacle and 60 years later comment- ed, "I lost the quarter I paid for the show."

I don't know who the ole boy was that said, "The show must go on," but if he had seen Theodore Lewis jack Grandpappy's jaw, he would have rephrased his words and said, "The show can't go on!"

Chapter 10

WHEN BASEBALL WAS KING

In the 1920s, there was little for young folks in Whittier to do. TVs, radios, computers and other gadgets that teenagers today take for granted, existed then only in a dream. Young boys and girls could catch a little play time outside if they had completed their chores. An old rope was handy; it could be slung across a branch and made into a tree swing--it gave a nice ride straight into the local swimming hole. Occasionally parents caught a medicine show or some singing entertainment. Folks needed rest from the hard work of the farm.

I doubt that, back then, people used the word "bored" very often. I also doubt that they missed the gadgets they never had. In Whittier, one man had a bright idea as well as the means to carry it out. Troy McLean was the depot agent in Whittier. He became interested in baseball. It's not for sure how he experienced his first game. The only media then was the radios, and they were still quite rare. There wasn't a way for folks in Whittier to watch baseball, so Troy decided to bring baseball to Whittier. In the 1920s there wasn't a telephone in Whittier, but there was a way to send a message; Troy McLean had a telegraph machine in his office down at the depot.

He began using his machine to contact other depot agents in Sylva, Murphy and Bryson City to schedule games. Interest spread quickly throughout the mountains as teams began to spring up all around.

In the 1920s, Whittier played and practiced at the end of Church Street. Little League ball was played in Whittier for at least fifty years until the 1970s, when Little League began to be played in Bryson City .

There were many good players back then. Periodically, a Little League Player moved up to the next level to play in high school, college or even a tryout with the Major Leagues. Bobby Game played in Whittier in the early 1950s and later went played for

When Baseball Was King

Western Carolina University. He tried out for the Baltimore Orioles but had injured his arm and didn't make the team. "He was a great pitcher," Doug Revis told me. No records are available to testify for his talent but his legend lives on in the memory of Doug Revis and others who saw him play.

William Wike's son, Mickey, played high school ball at Brevard. One night the coach had benched him because he was late for the game. It wasn't long before Bobby got a bright idea. He went walking through the stands, asking fans how much money they would pay him to slide into second base. He, of course, was supposed to be sitting on the bench. After he had gathered up the money, he started warming up. Late in the ninth inning, when the opposing batter was at the plate, Bobby went down on the field and got a running start. He then slid into home plate, nearly knocking the batter down. He did a victory dance, yelling and cheering wildly. His coach lit into him but Mickey went home with a pocketful of change.

In Whittier, the official overseer of the baseball field and gymnasium during the 1950s was Doug Revis. He lived next door, and if there was a game of any sort, be it basketball or baseball, he saw the players coming and joined in. Doug was quite a prankster then. One day, he became really creative. He got his old 8 track reel-to-reel player and ran a wire from his house to the sidewalk of the gym. When some young boy walked the sidewalk about dark, he d hear the ghost of Revis say, 'Hey you! What you doing?' The boy would then look around, but see nothing.

Baseball hit its peak in Whittier during the 1950s. Game day was a big event. The whole town looked forward to the evening games, except for the players. On game day, they knew that if the work on the farm wasn t done, then their dads wouldn't let them play. On other days they might have taken their time, but on game day, the hogs were slopped, the cows milked, and other chores completed in record time. No one dared miss playing in the big game.

The whole town came out for the baseball game. If it was a visiting team such as Cherokee or Bryson City, the rivalry was fierce. Everyone rooted for the Whittier hometeam. Stores closed, and often someone in the crowd would holler, 'I ll give you a quarter if you hit a home run!' The favorite snack at the baseball game wasn't beer and a hotdog as it is

My Mountain Granny

today, but peanuts mixed into an RC Cola.

In the mid 1950s someone had bought a set of lights for the field but they were never installed. Often the games didn't last until the ninth inning but ended when darkness fell.

Bats, balls and equipment were hard to come by because money was scarce. Fundraisers were often held to make money for the Little League teams. Donkey Ball games were sometimes played and raised many dollars that bought a bat, ball or glove for a young boy. One or two young boys would get on the donkey. One boy might ride on top and the other on the bottom side. Someone stood behind the donkey and gave it a little motivation. While it bucked about, the riders tried to hit the basket. I'm not sure if the participants practiced for Donkey Ball, but access to the gymnasium, wasn't by key. The ball players would crawl under the old gym and push up a loose board, then the fun would begin. I didn't find an official shooting percentage, but it was probably rather low.

Back then, baseball in Whittier was an official past time, but it meant more than that. Coach McLean , Curtis Revis and Doug Revis were great mentors. The young boys played hard, but played fair-

ly. No unsportsmanlike conduct was allowed, and no foul language or fighting were ever permitted. The young men worked hard and practiced the fundamentals. When the game was over, they shook hands with the other team. Young boys became men, and the game was a great way to teach values and character. The people of Whittier are fine folks. Baseball was a factor in molding the character of the people of Whittier.

When Baseball Was King

1969 Whittier Orioles

Front Row (Left to Right): Rick Wood, Eddie Sharp, Noonie Davis, Ricky Lossiah, Unknown, Lane Bailey, Unknown, James Sherrill, Joey Davis, and Ed Sheppard.

Back row (Left to Right): Jack Davis, Roane Garland, Buddy Lambert, Jerry Lossiah, Rick Lambert, Steve Lambert, Unknown, Dale Conner, Tim Hipps, Steve Whiddon, and Coach Doug Revis.

Chapter 11

INDIAN FRIENDS

"Can you talk Indian?" Evelyn asked me. She then began counting in Cherokee...

"Seowi, Tudli, Cheowi, Nicki, Hiski, Shoetudli, Telequa, Shoenell, Shanell, Skiheni. That's counting from one to ten in Indian. An old Indian lady taught me that.

"Near where we lived in Whittier was a trail that came from Birdtown down by our house. All of the Indians would walk to the stores. The women would carry their papooses, and just across the road from us, was this big ole sycamore tree. They would always stop and feed the children there. My sister and me went over and got acquainted with them. They taught us how to count to ten and how to say words. They was good to us, and we liked them. We learned to talk with them real good, and I never did forget that.

"They'd talk it real fast. I learned a lot of words but I've forgotten most of them. I still remember how to count."

Did you ever learn about native medicines from them?

" That was about all they did. Lord, let's see. What did we get out and hunt? Yellow root! Lord, we used to get out and hunt that up for the Indians. The Indians were good old people.

"I know we had one we laughed over him. He was a little short man, and he was a preacher. He preached over in Birdtown and had to go up by our house and cross over as he walked to church. He was a pastor over there, and every Sunday morning he'd come with his Bible under his arm, and then he'd come back that evening, drunk as a coot.

" If you offered liquor to the Indians, they would drink it. He came back that evening, a'staggering. His name was Uncle Davey Wetesut. He was a good old man, and everyone liked him. Maybe he didn't think it was wrong, I don't know. My sister and me got the biggest kick out of that. It would tickle us to death to see Uncle Davey Wetesut staggering around with a Bible under his arm after he had been at church all day. He must have just loved liquor.

"I can remember when hardly any of them could speak English. Julius, my husband, knew a lot of Indians because he worked in the stores. He waited on them, and to know what they wanted, you had to learn it.

"I can remember when the Indians were starving and came to my mama for meat skins. They could've farmed a little, but many didn't. Daddy always fattened a hog and Mama saved the meat skins for the Indians."

Chapter 12
RAYMOND ROBBINS

One afternoon I picked up a copy of the local newspaper. One of the articles was about a famous prohibition leader of the 1930's by the name of Colonel Raymond Robbins. The article made references to Whittier, N.C., so I visited Evelyn to find out if she had met Mr. Robbins.

When I met her that day, I handed her the article.

Did you know some man named Raymond Robbins? That article says he visited Whittier back in the 1930's.

She looked at me for a moment without speaking, her mind traveling back across the decades trying to recall a memory. Evelyn then began to smile really big.

" Well, of course I remember him. He was a big name then," she said.

How on earth did he end up here?

"Well, I don't know, but all of the children loved him. The adults didn't have a whole lot of time to do things with us. He played with us and was real good to us. I was so mad at Carl Byrd Fisher when he reported him. I liked him, and didn't want him to leave."

During the 1930's Colonel Raymond Robbins was very familiar to America. Robbins had become wealthy in the Klondike Gold Rush of 1898. He was a wealthy social worker and a leading prohibitionist who toured the country preaching against the evils of alcohol. Due to his efforts, he was on the front page of the newspaper regularly. Robbins was a close confidant of several U.S. presidents and was scheduled to meet with President Herbert Hoover just several days after his mysterious disappearance.

Raymond Robbins

President Hoover was alarmed that Robbins failed to appear at the important meeting and ordered an immediate investigation. Robbins' efforts against prohibition had made him many enemies, and threats on his life were common. Rumors were immediately flying, and the investigation made national headlines.

Meanwhile, the tiny mountain village of Whittier had a visitor. Whittier didn't see many foreigners back then. The mountains were very remote, and travel was difficult. A gentleman calling himself Reynold Rogers arrived on September 9, 1932, and began staying at the McHan Hotel. He was given a second-floor room for $5.00 a week. Not long after his arrival, he promised his landlord's daughter that he would send her to college.

Immediately Rogers became a part of the local community. He told people he was a prospector from, "up Kentucky way," looking for minerals in the area. Rogers was a fascinating speaker, and made political speeches. He talked frequently to groups at the hotel where he was staying. Rogers attended tribal meetings in Cherokee and took the local children on hikes. His arrival immediately raised speculation because Mr. Rogers' face was very familiar, even if the name

Robbins in Washington

he was using wasn't. He also had an education, something that was very rare in the local area.

Rogers enjoyed his new mountain home. Folks often saw him walking up Conley's Creek wearing a blue shirt and straw hat. He was known to walk twenty miles into the mountains. Three miles from Whittier on Battle Cove Knob, he found a tree he liked up on a knoll. At the top, he found an impressive view and would sit for hours staring into the far mountains.

The local children were delighted because he began taking them on hikes and giving them attention that the other adults were to busy to give them. He built a rustic outdoor theatre and began a series of Sunday entertainments in which he cast plays. The children loved Reynold Rogers.

One of those young children was a thirteen-year-old boy named Carl Byrd Fisher. He had seen Raymond Robbins' picture in the rural paper called the Grit. He recognized Mr. Rogers and wrote a letter to Colonel Robbins' Attorney in Chicago. He noted

My Mountain Granny

the resemblance and asked if there was a reward for locating Raymond Robbins. The following is that letter:

Whittier, NC
Nov. 11, 1932

Col. Solomon O. Levinson:

I believe that Col. Raymond Robbins is here at Whittier, and had been here for about seven weeks. His picture came out in the newspaper and I believe he is your man. He has a good education and is a world traveler.

When he came here he was slick shaven. Now he has a beard and wears an overall jacket. He says he was a personal friend of Teddy Roosevelt and knows President Herbert C. Hoover. He gives his name as Mr. R.H. Rogers.

Please send one of your men that knows him well or come yourself to Whittier, North Carolina. Please don't use my name in any report to the newspapers or give me away. If there are any rewards out here for finding him, please give it to me if he is the right man.

68

Hurry or several may see his picture and he may get away.

Carl Byrd Fisher
Whittier, NC

Folks who knew Robbins claimed he had great physical courage and tremendous sincerity. Fisher received his reward money, but its possible that he learned a little also from Robbins on those hikes in the woods. Fisher went on to become a World War II Veteran and Colonel himself.

Robbins' nephew, John Drier, and prohibition officer J. Ed Kanipe arrived in Whittier on Nov. 18, 1932. When the nephew questioned him, Robbins claimed he was Reynold Rogers.

Robbins in Whittier

"I am not your uncle," Robbins said.
"Yes, you are," his nephew replied.

Raymond Robbins

"I am not. You can bring President Hoover and his cabinet down here, and they will tell you that I am not the man!"

Robbins was the man, and he vanished as quickly as he had arrived. The Robbins discovery brought Whittier attention it was unaccustomed to. Newspaper men came and interviewed the postmaster and anyone who came in contact with Robbins and could recount a story about him.

Consequently his arrival at Appalachian Hall in Asheville for medical treatment also brought a flurry of media attention. He departed from Asheville to his home called "Chinsegut Hill" or "The Spirit of Lost Things." Robbins once said it was "the place where the things of true value that have been lost may be found again."

After he left Whittier, a letter was written with signatures mostly for school kids. They told Robbins how they missed him and wished he would visit. Later in life, Robbins made vague mentions to friends of a tiny town, two rivers, kindness and sunshine. One thing is certain: Whittier loved Reynold Rogers and Raymond Robbins loved Whittier.

Why did he come to Whittier? He was initially treated for amnesia, but later it was found he was keeping newspapers clippings related to his own disappearance. Colonel Raymond Robbins' life at the time was a blur of interviews and meetings. The prohibition effort was failing, and much of it he had funded, leaving his finances a mess. The storms were raging, and I suspect that as multitudes are doing today, Robbins decided he was through with the madness and escaped to the countryside for some down-home people in the North Carolina mountains.

Chapter 13
KANSAS AND TENNESSEE

My grandparents lived and raised their family of eleven children in the Qualla section of Jackson County. My grandfather's name was Kansas, and my grandmother's name was Tennessee. I always thought that was unusual. They lived in a large, two-story house and had many acres of land, a huge barn and a chicken house.

"Of course, he was a farmer and grew and raised most everything that they needed. His farm consisted of an apple and peach orchid, cherry trees and grape vineyards. I enjoyed all of that as a child. At that time there was no electricity in the rural areas. They had a good big spring with good water near the house so we carried pails and pails of water every day. All the family members took their baths in a big tin tub in the kitchen, which had a big fireplace, and in the Winter it was always burning.

"I loved to go see Grandma Howell but didn't want to go home. Uncle Dallas would get me on his back and take me to the barn to keep Mama from taking me home."

From where did the Howell's originate?

"They came out of Haywood County. Three brothers came from Wales and landed on the coast of North Carolina. One went West and the other, my great-grandfather, came to Western North Carolina. He owned a big plantation and had slaves.

"Granny Howell's grandmother was Granny Turpin. During the Civil War these soldiers came from Tennessee and stole her horses. Lord, she got on one and rode by herself over to Tennessee, around Gatlinburg. There wasn't even a road then. There was just a trail over the mountains. She got over and told the boss or captain about them stealing her horses.

"He said, 'Can you pick your horse out?'

Kansas and Tennessee

"She said, 'Sure, I can pick my horse out.'

"He took her out to the big corral, and she picked out her horses and led them back over the mountains herself. She wasn't afraid of nothing in the world. People survived and were tough, but they were good to one another.

"My Grandmother Varner lived to be eighty-six. Her mind was just as sharp and clear. In the summertime she'd sit out on the porch and read. Not many people her age could read. Back then people that old weren't educated. She was the only person that age in this country that could read. The mountains were backwards about getting things. She was up with things. Every one who walked by had to stop and talk to Grandma. She was a smart woman.

"My Granny Howell died when I was married. I was young, and I loved her to death. I thought it was the awfulest thing in the world when she died. When she died, they came and told me. That was my first experience I had with people dying close to me. I almost got mad at the Lord, you know. I'd think. 'That's not fair, that's not fair.' I had that type of feelings because I loved her to death. I thought she was the best woman in the world. She talked with a

brogue. I don't know how come she talked like that. When my momma would take my sister and me to her house, I never did want to leave. I'd go out crying 'I'm hungry.'

"Well, I wasn't hungry. I just wasn't wanting to leave. Granny would follow us way up the trail, with biscuits and sausage in her apron. She would follow us and say, 'No grandyoungin's gonna leave my house hungry.'

"I was around her more when I was young. I loved her to death.

One afternoon Evelyn took me to the old homeplace where we met Terry Howell, who also shared his remembrances of the homeplace:

"About 1914, they started building and they moved in here about 1917.

"Ya'll know who built this house? Grandpa commissioned Cam Hughs to build it, and when Cam got all through, he said, 'Now, Mr Howell, I've built you this house the best I know how to build it. I've got a favor to ask you. I'd like to marry your daughter!'

"There's never been a poisonous snake seen anywhere around here. Now you can shoot a rifle over

My Mountain Granny

there on that far mountain and they'll fan your britches with rattlers. For some reason, here in this valley there are no poisonous snakes. Nobody ever seen a rattler in this valley.

"Will Thomas was the only white man that was ever chief of the Cherokee. They called him 'Little Will.' Over there in Whittier, as you started up towards, up the river, he lived up there a little ways. Part of that's still the original house. See, in 1837, they declared the Indians outlaws here and took some of them to Oklahoma, but the Indians left here gave money to Will, who bought land in his name.

"His granddaughter went to college up in Pennsylvania with Jim Thorpe.

"There was an old Indian named Gudger who didn't speak. I said, 'You didn't learn much of that did you?'

"He said, 'No, Grandpa never would teach me how to speak Indian. When I went to Columbia University, if they caught us speaking Indian they washed our month out with Octagon soap. What they were trying to do was make us blend with the white people.

"Gene Alley Turpin was a year older than me and

he'd whip the waddin' out of me every evening. So I came by down there one evening, and I thought, 'I'm gonna fix me a thorny stick, and I'm gonna get him tomorrow.'

"Dad came by and said, 'What are ye a'doin' there?'

"I said, 'I'm fixing me a thorny stick, and I'm gonna take care of Gene Alley Turpin tomorrow.'

"He said, 'He'll take that stick away from you and beat Hell out of you.'

"So the next day I went to school with my stick but I made a mistake. I told someone about it. Gene Alley knew about the stick that evening. He beat me good. I had a black eye when I came home and Dad looked at me and said, 'I told you he'd beat Hell out of you.'"

"And what would parents say today? Lets go talk to his mama!'"

The Stock Market crashed on October 29th, 1929 and a dark cloud spread across the political and economic landscape of America. The Great Depression cast doubt and despair into the soul of America. Herbert Hoover, the 31st president of the United States was in office when the Depression began. He had been president for only seven months, just long enough to warm his chair in the Oval Office, and the Depression was tossed upon him.

Hoover was a remote, grim-faced man who shied away from public attention. When he did something noteworthy, he refused to use it for political gain and failed to win a mandate for his programs.

America needed a cheerleader such as the great communicator, Ronald Reagan. We needed someone to inspire America, to kick down the door of poverty

and find hope for a better day. America, instead, had Hoover. It's easy to point the finger and cast blame. Hoover didn't cause the crash and the beginning of the Depression, but his administration made several errors which only made the situation worse.

Americans look to their president for reassurance in difficult times. At a time when unemployment had reached twenty-five percent and the stock market had fallen eighty-nine percent, he assured prosperity was on the way, while people were starving to death.

Americans, indeed, were starving, with no hope of a job, a meal or an education. Hoover clung to the theory of rugged individualism. He held to a policy of limited government, believing that government intervention stifled creativity and initiative. He was seen as cold and uncaring. He once said, "A dollar a day and a pair of overalls were enough for any man." The trouble was most men couldn't find a dollar, and many had no clothes to wear. Americans were bitter and looking for a scapegoat on whom to dump their frustrations. President Hoover had done little to help his cause.

What could a man do if he was without a home? He had a cardboard shack and lived in run-down shanty town called a Hooverville. If he was without food, he either rummaged through garbage looking for a crumb of bread, or ate an armadillo, commonly called a Hoover-hog. Folks were angry that Hoover had broken his promise of a chicken in every pot. If a man was jobless, he hopped aboard a rail car and became a hobo riding a Hoover-Pullman. If he was cold, he stuffed newspapers in his jacket and called them Hoover-blankets. Folks turned their pockets inside out and called them Hoover-flags, proclaiming "Brother, can you spare a dime?"

On the campaign trail in 1932, Hoover was laughed at, booed and had tomatoes thrown at his train. Hoover lost the election by an astounding 472 to 59 in electoral votes to incumbent Franklin Delano Roosevelt. He left office as the most hated man in America.

Hoover lived thirty years after leaving office just long enough to see his vision fade into a new era of socialism started by his successor, Franklin D. Roosevelt.

Roosevelt become the 32nd president of the United States. Roosevelt took office on March 4, 1933 and thus began one of the most profound changes in

Great Depression

American history. It has been said that the night after the inauguration, the lights in the Oval Office burned all night. Roosevelt hit the ground running. He had a plan and introduced his "New Deal" for America.

It's true that, if a man is given a handout, he usually asks for more once its gone. Roosevelt's "New Deal" was brilliant. It provided for people who needed food, clothing, healthcare, education and shelter, without a handout. They worked for their relief and built valuable infrastructure.

The major parts of his program were relief agencies such as the Works Progress Administration and the Civilian Conservation Corp.

Roosevelt and Hoover had opposite visions for America. Hoover believed against government intervention and was against change, while Roosevelt believed in sweeping changes that would lift America up.

In Jackson County the Depression forced political change. It resulted in a complete shift from Republican to Democratic, as it did in most of the nation. The combined efforts of the WPA and CCC were a shot in the arm to the local economy. There were no jobs and no money in the county. Blackwood Lumber Company went down overnight as it depended on the furniture building industry.

Farming grew unprofitable as prices dropped drastically. Sylva Paper Company was a bright spot. It survived pretty well with only a couple of slowdowns in '36 and '39. If a man was to find work, it commonly paid seventy-five cents a day. People had plenty of goods from the farm but no money, so often wages would be paid in corn, potatoes or meat. Families scratched out a living as all worked, including the kids.

Bartering was a means of survival. Every store had a cow lot or chicken coop. Families could take their livestock and trade for what they needed. A hundred pounds of cabbage was worth about 50 cents and could be traded for a 25lb bag of flour. A dozen eggs could be traded for a yard of cloth.

My Mountain Granny

Nationally, a large number of banks failed. Jackson County had two banks when the Depression started. The Tuckaseegee Bank had been in its marble building on Main Street a year when disaster struck. In April of 1930 the banking institution was forced to close. There was an investigation and several officials were indicted for receiving deposits knowing the bank was insolvent. The bank was liquidated, and depositors got ten cents on the dollar. Many lost from a few cents to 1000's of dollars. A storekeeper, named J.P. Haskett, was told by officials that he couldn't get his money. He kicked the bank door down in anger.

Farming in the 30's

The Jackson County Bank weathered the Depression in good condition. The story goes that C.J. Harris went to Wachovia Bank in Asheville and got a large amount of cash. He

laid it in full view of the customers who had come to receive deposits and said, "Here's your money. Come and get it."

The Works Projects Administration had a major impact on the county. In 1934, 125 men in the county had work through the WPA. Work relief projects covered a wide range from sewing rooms for women to heavy construction. The WPA built the wall below the courthouse and built several buildings at WCU. They built schools, had literacy classes and provided trade schools for some. The products women made in the trade schools such as clothing, mattresses, etc. went to local families. The WPA also did local projects. They built outhouses for families and did individual projects. If the family could pay, the money went back to the WPA fund.

The school lunch benefit program for relief clients through the WPA is now taken for granted. It provided at least one adequate meal per day for under-nourished children and gave parents an education in nutrition. It operated in eleven schools, and teachers reported a difference in attendance and grades.

Children who had one or two miles to walk to

school were absent on all but the most pleasant days. A hot meal increased school attendance. With a hot lunch, attendance was up. WPA workers canned thousands of quarts of food for lunchrooms.

As was the custom before government welfare, churches and local groups organized to care for the needy. In 1928, the Baptist and Methodist churches organized a welfare committee to provide clothes and food for people out of work.

The local mountains hadn't known much prosperity when the Depression began. In 1930, ten percent of the homes in Jackson County had electricity. Most people farmed on a small scale, fattening a hog, keeping a cow for milk and butter, and raising a big garden. Everyone hunted and one local man reported he didn't see a live deer until he was much older, because they were all on the dinner plate. Folks here survived better than those in the city because they had land to farm and had the know how to survive in hard times. Roosevelt had fireside chats with America and proclaimed that, "The only thing we have to fear is fear itself."

America took its first steps toward Socialism. Roosevelt instituted many reforms aimed at making life better. He established social security, collective bargaining, disability benefits, shorter work weeks and better working conditions. He gave America the hope of a better tomorrow. If it's true that turmoil is fertile ground for change, The Great Depression produced more change for a better America than any other period in American History.

Evelyn, can you tell me about your experience with the Great Depression ?

"I grew up during the Depression. The only food we had then was what Daddy grew and Momma put up. The corn was especially good. We had enough potatoes to go all year round. I didn't know what it was like to buy potatoes in a store.

"People during that time didn't buy anything new. What you didn't have, you did without. What hurt me the worst during that Depression was we couldn't buy toothpaste and I had to use baking soda. That came within an ace of breaking my heart.

"Mr. Rhodes had a store down there, and his wife couldn't sew. She'd get Mama to make her children's dresses. Mama would take that money and buy

My Mountain Granny

material to make me and my sister dresses.

"Daddy was a railroad man, and he had a job longer than most of them. The year that I was a senior, he got laid off. I was a senior in high school and made real good grades. I remember Mama saying each morning, 'Evelyn, we just can't send you to school.' I'd act like I just didn't hear her and I'd get ready and catch the bus. In April, just before I graduated, Daddy got hired with Georgia Power and Light. He stayed there until he retired. What if I'd up and quit school? There wasn't a bit of use in that. I done had everything to wear to school. I reckon Mama felt I was the only one that didn't have nothing. My Lord, nobody had anything.

"Daddy owned a milk cow and fattened a hog, and we had our own meat.

"The Woods family, who lived down below us, had four boys, but they didn't have a milk cow. Lord, he was a carpenter but couldn't get a day's work. Nobody built anything during the Depression. Every afternoon Mamma would fix a bucket. She'd say, 'I can't stand for those children not to have any milk.' We would walk down there every evening about supper time and take milk for the little boys.

The little town of Whittier

"The food part of the Depression never bothered us. We just couldn't go to the store and buy nothing. We fared better than a lot of people. Mama was a real good seamstress. Now, I never did master that. She could take a piece of cloth and make us the prettiest dresses in the world. Ya know, it didn't cost much. We made a great big garden, a corn patch, had a hog and we had our own milk and butter. During the Depression Mama sold milk and butter. We just about lived at home. Mama always had good meals.

"People have more needs now than back then. If you had a clean dress to put on and a pair of shoes back then, you were happy. Most of the children knew

Great Depression

Daddy bought one pair of shoes a year, and that's all they had. You came in from school, and the first thing you did was pull off that dress and shoes. You put on an old something cause during that Depression, you couldn't get no more of them.

"Most of the youngin's went barefooted. I never did much like to go barefooted. We always had new shoes and dresses when school started. I think people were happier when they didn't have so much. People loved one another, and they got along good. If someone got sick, the neighbors all pitched in and helped out if they needed it. There wasn't no money but it was a good time.

"Everyone had to have something to feed their family. Some stole, but if I had to I'd rather make liquor than steal. You learned how to manage. We had food, clothes, and we were always warm. It was bad, but it could have been worse.

"Daddy always liked to take the paper, and the man who lived above us always liked to take the paper. We had no money. Mr. Rogers said, 'Listen, how about you get it in the morning and put it back in the box at 12:00, and I'll get it in the afternoon and we'll each pay half.' We always had the paper.

"I understood the Depression and I blamed it on Herbert Hoover. I said, 'I'll never vote another old Republican ticket...I'll not do it. I'm 82 years old, and I ain't never voted a Republican ticket. Daddy and all of the Howells were Republicans, but I never voted a Republican ticket. I couldn't stand old Herbert Hoover's picture. I'd see his picture, and I'd take a pencil or knife and poke holes in it. He might have been a real good man, but I blamed it all on him.

"In a way, to grow up during the Depression, we had the best time in the world. We had a real good time. Well, it was hard times. We didn't have money, but now Dr. Tidmarsh lived right down there in Whittier. He was our doctor. If the youngin's or anybody got sick he went to see them. If they didn't have no money, that was all right. He took care of all the people."

Chapter 15
SCHOOL DAYS

Tell me about your school days, Evelyn.

"I went to Whittier Grade School until I finished the seventh grade and had never been happier in my life. I really loved school in spite of the fact that my first day at school, when I wouldn't obey the teacher, she put a circle on the blackboard and made me stand with my nose pressed into it. I told my mother I wasn't going back to school, but I did. I was bossy and often played teacher, telling other students what to do.

"I got in trouble several times when I'd come back at my teachers. They'd make me stay and write something 100 times. I made real good grades, and I knew if I kept my grades up, they wouldn't do much with me. I could get by with a lot. I was real fidgety

and never stayed still in my seat. I didn't do no bad things. I was up sharpening my pencil and wondering if I'd get in trouble, but they let me do that because I made real good grades.

"Miss Mae was a small woman with long pretty hair. She had such a good easy way with children, as she was the second grade teacher for a great number of years.

"She was teaching at the same school I was a substitute teacher. Miss Mae walked up and down the hill to school each day. She didn't hold with riding to school. One thing I recall about her: she dearly loved onion sandwiches.

"One morning she came in the room just in time for the bell to ring. She went to the cloak room to take off her coat. She had on a real pretty blouse, but when she looked down, she saw her petticoat. She had forgotten to put on her skirt. I never wanted to laugh as much in all my life as at that moment, but my manners wouldn't let me. Somehow, I kept a serious look on my face. Miss Mae said, 'Evelyn, will you watch my students while I go home and get my skirt? Please don't let the principal know about this.'

"'Of course,' I told her. 'Yes, Miss Mae. I'll be happy to watch your students.'

"The principal never knew. Miss Mae's students learned real well, but she and the principal didn't see eye-to-eye on all issues. She never failed to let him know how she felt and believed, which of course didn't always go over good with him.

"When she retired, Miss Mae had not married. I don't think that she had many beauxs either, but she wanted to travel and wanted to travel. So travel she did.

"Somewhere in Texas, she met and married a rich elderly man. Her friends

"WHAT a child learns is important, but how he grows while he learns it is more important . . . ."

"THE PURPOSE of EDUCATION is to effect changes in conduct on the part of the person educated. Only that child has been truly educated during a term, a year, or any other period of time, whose conduct has been materially changed at the end of that period, as measured by his conduct at the beginning."

. SWAIN COUNTY

PUBLIC SCHOOL RECORD

Monthly Report of

Evelyn Howell

A Pupil in _____*Tenth*_____ Grade

_____*Swain County High*_____ School

The _____*Charleston*_____ School District

Year 193__ - 193__

The pupil above, having met the requirements of the grade, is hereby _____ promoted to *Tenth* grade

Lillian Wheeler
Teacher

_____
Principal

Date _____*April 19, 1933*_____

almost went into shock when they learned. I do believe Miss Mae was one of the happiest and most unusual people I have ever met.

"We walked to school at Whittier because we didn't have buses until we went to Swain County High School. I liked all my teachers from 1st to 7 th grade at Whittier. It was a country school. The boys would jump out of the window when the teachers got onto them. They would go up Cemetery Hill and sit on a hill all evening. The teacher knew they'd out-run her, and she'd get them later. I'd worry about them. What fun was that? I'd rather be sitting there in the schoolhouse.

The 7th grade was the first time ever we had a man teacher. His name was Ervin Crawford, and we gave him a fit. Everyone in the room was afraid of him except me.

81

My Mountain Granny

Whittier in the 1930's
Evelyn Graduated in 1935

I made good grades, but, boy, did I give him a fit! His girl-friend came to the door and I peeked through the key-hole to see who it was. He opened the door, and I fell in the floor. I think it tickled him, but he couldn't laugh. He said, 'Evelyn, curiosity killed the cat and if you're not careful it will kill you, too.' The room just roared.

"Not too long ago, my sister ran into him over there in Asheville. He said, 'Listen, I want to talk to you. What kind of adult did your sister make? I've wondered and wondered about that.'

"My sister said, 'Believe it or not, she has done pretty well.'

"I had a great time in high school and never had to take any examinations. They would post exemptions on the big board in the hall. I made good grades, and that's why I got by with so much. They'd put exceptions on the big board out in the hall with my name on it, and that would thrill me to death.

" I was happy in high school and I know the year I come up to graduate, but I lacked a science. Physics was the one class in high school everybody dreaded, and they told me I'd have to go in that class. Well, I cried, because I thought that would knock me out of graduating. The funniest thing was I got in there, and I ate it up. I was exempt both semesters. I liked it better than anything I ever studied. We had the sweetest teacher in the world. Mrs. Daniels was her name. They posted that big exemption board in the big hall, and there was my name, Evelyn Howell. I was surprised because I had no idea that I could ever pass it.

"I know I got into big trouble one time. Eight of us girls at Swain County High School got an idea. There was three or four CCC camps at Smokemont. We got together and decided we would stay out of school and go to the CCC camps. We thumbed our way up there.

"The mechanic up at the CCC camps was on the school board, and we didn't know it. Lord, the next morning we went in, and our names were called. We had to go to the office. We worked till school got out, and we didn't get recess or nothing.

"What in the world made us do that? Lord, our parents about killed us.

"My daddy was a railroad man, and the year I was about to graduate, he got laid off. They kept him longer than anyone else because he was good and dependable.

"The rest of the kids had to drop out of school, but I'd rather have gone to school. I liked to go to school. Mama made me work, and I was lazy. I was better in school because Mama believed in working every minute.

"When I went, people couldn't finish school. They had to help their mamma and daddy. I went on and finished in 1935. Twenty-four finished Whittier Grade School and four of those finished high school. I graduated with Martha Allen, Haven Davis, and Hal McClain. Haven was quiet, and he'd say, 'Evelyn, hush! You're going to get us into trouble.' I had to wash blackboards a lot for punishment.

"I graduated high school on a Sunday morning with 64 people in my graduating class. We had our cap and gown and walked to the stage to get our diplomas. I was very fortunate to graduate.

" I got married two weeks later, although Julius wanted to get married that night. I said, ' Flip, I'm too tired to get married. I'm going home.'"

Chapter 16

LOVE OF A LIFETIME

So, Evelyn, you married right out of high school!

"I fell in love for the first and only time when I met my husband-to-be, Julius Beck. He was a handsome, older man. I met him on Easter Sunday, 1934, at the Church of God in Whittier. My heart would beat real fast every time I saw him. He was the most mature person I'd ever seen and was ten years older than me. I'd had other boyfriends around my own age but he was special, and I didn't date anyone after we met.

"On our dates we usually went to movies, church, took walks and went to parties. Christmas Day, 1934, Julius proposed and said, 'Let's get married next week.'

Evelyn and Julius shortly after marriage

"At this time married women couldn't attend school. 'I'm gonna finish school,' I replied. 'It's only three months from now.'

"After I graduated from Swain County High School, Julius and I were married at the court house in Clayton, Georgia, on May 11th. He was twenty-seven, and I was seventeen.

"Neighbors had predicted I would ruin my life,

and had scolded my mother for letting us date. Julius wore a burgundy suit, and I wore a light blue dress with a white bow. I remember being scared to death on my wedding day, but we had sixty years of happy life together until his death."

How did you meet him, especially since he was so much older than you?

" I had been noticing him go up the road by the house. I kept a'wondering who was that? He had coal black eyes, black hair and was dark-skinned. One day later, I was sitting on the porch getting my homework. He walked over and said, 'What are you doing? I've been a'wantin' to get acquainted with you, but I haven't had a chance. Will you be at the service tonight?' That started it...we never broke up nor had a fuss.

"He walked me home that night, and I fell for him. Julius was in Whittier because he was staying with his sister, Velma, who lived above us. I thought he was the best-looking man I had ever laid eyes on.

"Everyone gave me a hard time over it. I was too young; he was older than me. My parents, they didn't want me to marry him. Daddy was nicer to him than Mama. When she met him, he was sewing his wild oats. He made a change and became a Deacon. He was getting ready to settle down and wanted someone decent. He came from a well-thought-of family with no trash or nothing.

"Oh, that was a big topic with everybody in a little community...everybody tried in every way to keep me from going with him. Julius and me would slip off because Mom and Dad never let me go anywhere with him. I'd pretend to go church, and I'd go with him.

" Julius asked me to marry him while we were at his sister's. We sat down on the porch and talked. He wanted to marry at Christmas, but I said, 'I'm not marrying at Christmas. I'm gonna finish school'"

"He said, 'Well, that's alright. I'll just go back to West Virginia.'

"I said, ' Well, that's alright if that's what you want to do...then just go back up there and work.'

"I didn't really want to marry him then, but I didn't want no other woman to have him either. I wasn't around him a lot because he worked and I was in school. I had dated him my whole senior year. He'd been with blacktopping in West Virginia. and I thought he was gone. I went on to school and was gonna forget about him. Lord, on Wednesday night, in the gate he came."

Did he ask your daddy for your hand in marriage?

"He didn't want to tell Daddy, but finally he had to. He said, 'Mr. Howell, me and Evelyn's gonna get married tomorrow.'

"Daddy told him, 'Well, if that's the way it's gonna be, then that's the way it will be. But you had better treat her right and do her good, son.'

"We got married in May, right after I graduated. Most of them would go to the pastor's house and marry. My husband and me went to Georgia. I was underage, and Mama and Daddy wouldn't sign for me. In Georgia, they had different laws, so we went over there and got married. We got along the best; he never did leave me...I never did leave him.

Evelyn in her 20's

"Lord, that was a big trip for me...going to Clayton, GA. I had never been that far before.

"Georgia was a long trip in those days. We were on our way, and Dan Honeycut, who was driving, told me as we approached the Georgia line, 'Evelyn I hope you don't mind but I need you to do something for me.'

"I said 'Well, what is it? I don't mind at all.'

"He said, 'It's illegal for me to transport a minor across the state line. I need you to get out and walk into Georgia.'

"I got out of the car on the North Carolina side and walked across the state line. I wore a pale blue dress, and we were married by a Justice of the Peace, M.H. James. Our witnesses were Dan Honeycut and his wife, Tillitha.

"We came back and stayed at Velma's, who was Julius's sister. Lord, back then no one had ever heard of a honeymoon trip. People didn't have no money to go.

"I married at seventeen, and then you had to be 21

86

to vote. It was a long time before I was old enough to vote. I thought, 'Well I'm not gonna live with no man and vote agin him.'

"My husband never said a word. I guess he won-dered what I was gonna do. I went out and voted a Democratic tick-et. If he had said, 'You're gonna vote with me,' I wouldn't have done it. I had registered Democrat because he was a Democrat. I made up my own mind, and he did not say one word.

Baby Joyce

"We rent-ed at Smokemont when we were on road jobs. When we came back, we bought that place on Shoal Creek. That was the first place we ever bought. When we were on road jobs, we were going place to place continually all the time. We couldn't own a house doing that. When the job got done, he was gone.

"We were in Pennsylvania and he told me that we had to be gone by 6:00 am the next morning for a job in North Carolina. I had to pack my clothes and get gone.

"We were living in Highlands, and Julius was on a road job. Julius broke his leg out on the job. They didn't tell me until Julius was at the hospital. I had to move everything back to Whittier. I walked into the Home Cash Store and started crying, 'We don't have nothing. I just don't know how we're gonna make it.'

"My uncle owned the Home Cash Store. He told me, ' Now Evelyn, you can have everything in the store that you want. We here in Whittier are gonna see that you make it. I know you will pay me back.'

"I took the bull by the horns and rented a room.

"This was a very trying time because I had a new baby during all of this. Julius was in Angel Hospital in Franklin. They kept him and kept him. Soon we figured out why they were keeping him. The company was paying for it, and no one could pay a bill during the Depression. I went in and didn't say a word to anyone at the hospital. I put him in a wheelchair, took him to the car and got him out of there.

"When Joyce came along, that changed things. I told him, 'Now listen, you can go on all the road jobs you want to. I'm not gonna raise this child from hand-to-mouth. She's gonna be raised in a stable house and have some roots'. That's when he quit construction work.

"Julius was on that job where they were building the road from Bryson City to Topton. We lived there in Nantahala. I'd like to tell you what them crazy old men did. The rock crusher was above where we lived, and all the men who worked there had cabins and lived close together.

"They would send us to Topton to buy liquor, and we would bring it back to them. They didn't get drunk or nothing, but on the job, they'd take a drink. They'd

Mama's Girl

give us money because everyone in Topton made liquor, and we hauled it back in the car. I wouldn't do that now for nothing. If we had got caught, they would have paid us out.

"Everyone up there bootlegged. There weren't any jobs so you about had to do it to survive. There was no such thing as welfare. You just starved if you didn't have nothing.

"I'd fly mad in an instant then, but it was quick and it was over with. I never held a grudge in my life. We ran a store a few years later down there in Whittier. We had groceries, drinks, and ice cream but we had a

88

good business in there.

"I remember one time when I was as hateful as I could be. Ice cream was classed as a food, and there wasn't a tax on food. But we had to pay the tax. (I still think I was right.) Julius didn't open his mouth. He wasn't as brave as I was. I tore into him, and my husband just stood there with his eyes right big.

"No, the tax collector didn't give no notice at all. He just showed up at the front door. I pitched a fit on him. I told that tax collector, 'Now just take the whole stock of stuff and get out, just take it and get out.' Julius thought I was going to get us put in jail.

"Julius was a good worker, dependable and honest. He always had a job. We were married sixty-two years and I don't think he was ever without a job. He was a good man, and I never was sorry I married him.

"Julius had a real bad stroke and he stayed in the nursing home for four years. That was the most stressful thing to me, not knowing when I left that day, if he would be alive the next. I left here sometimes with snow on the road, but I never missed a Saturday. I never bellyached one time."

Chapter 17

SMOKEMONT

The Civilian Conservation Corp was a vital part of President Franklin D. Roosevelt's New Deal program. Its purpose was to breathe life into an economically-depressed nation. Men were put to work building roads, bridges, parks and other necessary projects. Thus, poor families found work and steady income while building infrastructure that would be vital to the future of our nation.

The Civilian Conservation Corp was one of Franklin D. Roosevelt's alphabet agencies. America was in the grip of the Great Depression when Franklin Delano Roosevelt was inaugurated in March of 1933. Twenty-five percent of the population was unemployed, and hungry. These were desperate times, and the program gave hungry young men hope.

Roosevelt's platform included conservation work

as unemployment relief during his presidential campaign. On May 7, Roosevelt promoted the CCC in a fireside address.

"First, we are giving opportunity of employment to one-quarter of a million of the unemployed, especially the young men who have dependents, to go into the forestry and flood prevention work. This is a big task because it means feeding, clothing and caring for nearly twice as many men as we have in the regular army itself. In creating this Civilian Conservation Corp we are killing two birds with one stone. We are clearly enhancing the value of our natural resources and second, we are relieving an appreciable amount of actual distress."

The CCC and WPA were all part of Roosevelt's "New Deal" program.

The CCC was actually run and organized by the Army. Though it was a non-military operation, Fort McPherson, Georgia, was the command post for district B, which had 28 work camps in north Georgia, North Carolina, and upstate South Carolina. Officers, noncommissioned officers, and privates were called off their regular duties for temporary duty organizing and running the CCC camps.

The CCC had two main purposes. One was the conservation of our natural resources. One of the major tasks of the corps was refor-estation. Much of the land in north Georgia and throughout the Southeast had been stripped bare.

This land was bought at bargain prices by the U. S. government and became part of the CCC mission.

Secondly, it was to stimulate the economy by giving young men

Standing outside the mess hall waiting for the dinner bell to be rung. Note the big metal triangle waiting to be struck.

The most popular building in camp was the mess hall. There were about twenty tables at which some two hundred men were served.

Taken from "CCC Days" by Frank Davis

jobs. This put money into their pockets and back into the economy. They learned a trade and performed public service. This gave them skills that they could use, when their two-year term of enlist-ment was over.

Members lived in camps, wore uniforms, and lived under military discipline. They had inspections, Army clothing and Army rules They even had initiations as in the Army. Upon entering, seventy percent were under-fed and poorly-clothed. Very few had more than a year of high school education. Some were so weak from hunger upon arrival, they could bare-ly stand up without leaning on a shovel. They lived in wooden barracks, rising when the bugle sounded at 6:00 am, reporting to work by 7:45, and working until 4:00 pm

The CCC had military-style punishments. Extra duty on KP was common for infractions such as shoes not being shined, a shirt being unbuttoned or bed not made up. On weekends there was bus service to town, or they could attend dances or religious services in the camp. Discipline was maintained by the threat of "dishonorable discharge."

"This is a training station and we're going to leave morally and physically fit to lick Old Man Depression ," boasted a North Carolina newsletter.

During its time, there were many nicknames for the Civilian Conservation Corps, but the most common, by far, was "Roosevelt's Tree Army." This name stuck because the recruits were young men who "enrolled" for a term of service, and lived in "camps" much like the Army.

In the 1930s, it was common for students to quit before graduating high school because they were breadwinners in the family. There was less emphasis on formal education because most Americans earned their living from agriculture. Each camp had a C.E.A., Camp Education Advisor. It was his responsibility to design lessons for any enrollee who wanted to use his free time to further his education. Programs ranged

C.C.C. Co. 411-N.C. N.P.-5, Camp Kephart Prong. Smokemont, N.C.

Smokemont

from basic elementary skills, to college-level classes. Education made a difference in the CCC boys. It is said that approximately forty thousand men learned how to read and write. A CCC classroom was located anywhere that you could find a chair, or a tree stump. Subjects covered a wide range of vocational endeavors. Truck driving, mechanics, cooking, furniture building, forestry, masonry, road construction, dam building, and conservation techniques were all part of the public service projects of the New Deal. Thousands went to night school in the community.

The only requirements to be enrolled in the CCC were to be 18 years of age and that, of the $30 monthly pay, $25 be sent home to the person's family. After observing the new standard eight-hour day and five-day work week at manual labor, the enrollees could, if they wanted, attend evening classes at different educational levels to study subjects ranging from college-level U.S. history and civics classes to basic literacy. Skilled courses such as motor repair, cooking, and baking were also taught. As the unemployment rate fell, so did the need for the CCC. The CCC lost importance as the Depression ended. Rather than formally disbanding the CCC, Congress ceased funding it after 1942, causing it to end operations.

Tell us about your life in Smokemont, Evelyn.

"It was in the middle of the nineteen thirties, that I went to live in the small village of Smokemont, N.C. It was nestled in the small valley, surrounded by mountains. The Oconaluftee river ran down the center of the village. There was no electricity or indoor plumbing. I didn't miss it, as I had never had it. We had no telephone, but we had a good life with very little pressure about anything. There was one church, and it still stands today. All the people of the village went to it.

"We had two grocery stores. George Beck owned one and J. Hugh Conner owned the other, with the Post Office in the side. It was located about a half-mile down the road.

"There were three Civilian Conservation Corp camps nearby, so we never felt isolated or lonely. Many people were around us all the time. The CCC boys had lots of entertainment at the camps and we were invited to many social events. In fact, I enjoyed going to the big square dances with the good music. It was a happy time in my life, but at the time, I didn't realize it.

"The summers were best of all in the Great Smoky Mountains. We had various ball teams and a good nearby swimming hole, just below the bridge that leads to the campground. I hardly missed a day going swimming there during July and August. There were never any really hot days in the summer then, and we had lots of trails for walking. Winters were cold with lots of snow. I read a lot of books during the winter months and also learned to quilt and crochet.

" There was one warden assigned to our district. We all knew and liked him very much. He was all the law enforcement we had, but we didn't seem to need him very much. I had never heard of dope and much of the other things in our society today. The men were working for thirty or forty dollars a month. There were no jobs for women, but I look on that as a good time. It was so pretty in the spring with lots of wildflowers everywhere you looked.

"My husband and I spent the first three years of our married life there. I am thankful for all the good memories I have of the little place called Smokemont."

Baby Joyce arrived in 1938. She had dark blue eyes and jet black hair. I thought she was the prettiest baby I had ever seen. I fed, bathed her, and changed her diapers. Soon, the shadow of war became a reality, and Julius was drafted. I was lonely living alone with a small child. Joyce and I played games by the fire on winter evenings, and in the summer we swam. My little girl came into the world with coal black hair, wrinkled and red. She was a new experience for me. I didn't know what to do with her when she cried, fussed, or wouldn't sleep, but oh, how I loved her. She was a survivor, and I did learn how to take care of her.

"Joyce was also a great comfort to me when her daddy went off to World War II. We had a Christmas alone, and she was so surprised that Santa Claus came to see her with her daddy away.

" She started to school when she was five and

acted like she had gone every day of her life. Some of the children cried and she called me over to her little desk and said, 'Momma, why are they crying?' I knew then that she was going to be fine. She never would eat oatmeal for breakfast, but her teacher told her the healthy aspects of oatmeal. She came to me and said, 'Momma please make me some oatmeal for my breakfast.' I was so surprised, but happy to learn that her teacher was influencing her that way.

Joyce took clogging and dancing in all of the elementary grades and got very good at it. Once, she danced with Jim Nabors at a concert, and of course I

My Mountain Granny

felt very proud of her. I think having a little girl is one of the best and sweetest experiences of my life. I wish I had six girls instead of one. I enjoyed every phase of my little girl's life. I have sweet memories to draw on for which I am so thankful.

"My sister's boy's name was Ralph Eugene. Then the doctor couldn't tell you what you were gonna have. I didn't know if it was going to be a boy or girl. Ralph Eugene was the name Julius and I had picked out, if it was gonna be a boy. With Joyce, I waited a good long while to come up with a name. I thought, 'Joyce sounds good. We'll name her that, if it's a girl.'

"I wasn't in labor but one hour. The doctor barely got in the door, and Joyce was born. He said, 'I never seen nothing to beat that in my life.' He stayed mad at me as long as he lived, because I didn't have no more children. He said, 'Anybody that has a baby as quick as you did and don't have no more, shame, shame on you.' I said, 'Everything I've done in my life I've done in a hurry'.' To me that was no big thing.'

"She weighed seven pounds. She looked a little like an Indian girl when she was little. Julius had coal black hair, black eyes and dark skin. When I was pregnant, I got out and climbed over fences and did any-

thing I wanted to do. I went right on like I always did. 'Evelyn, you'll have trouble. It's gonna kill you or that baby one,' my friend said. I guess all that exercise was good. Dr. Bateman said that was the quickest first delivery he'd ever seen in his life. I ran up hills and all over yonder. I reckon everyone thought that when you were pregnant, you laid down or sat down, one or the other.

"When Joyce was little, we had this drunk that would come by the house hollering all the time. Glen Norman was his name, and he came out there hollering, waking my baby up. I went out there, and I made a believer out of him. I pointed my gun right at him, and said, 'Glen I just have a big mind to shoot your head off. I'm tired of you waking my baby up.'

"'Oh, God, Evelyn, put that gun up!' he screamed. But you bet, from then on he'd go by my house just as quiet. I wouldn't have shot him. I think I scared him sober.

"Mama never let us girls go nowhere. It was all ball games and school activities. We let Joyce go to all kinds of things. There was some places we didn't let her go, but she never did much ask to go to those places. She was in school and church activities. She

96

never was a problem."

What values did you try to teach your child?

" I tried to instill in Joyce, 'Tell the truth, don't never tell a lie! Be truthful if you do nothing else.'
" I don't reckon Joyce ever told me a story.
"My husband worked at the prison camp. I'd take Joyce up there, when she was about four, to visit Julius. Those prisoners petted her to death. They'd save things to give her when I took her up there. They loved Joyce and petted her because they never got to see little children."

Chapter 19
THE FLOOD OF 1940

In that era, no one had heard of TVs, and many folks didn't have a radio or a telephone. With regard to natural disasters, there was no warning system like we have today.

Whittier in the 1940 Flood

On that day in August of 1940, the mighty Tuckaseegee roared, washing away everything in its path. From Little Canada, Cullowhee, and Dillsboro, in Jackson County to Whittier and Bryson City, every highway bridge was washed away. Four people were killed, 34 homes and many businesses were washed away. Despite the force of the river, there was no warning. The river rose fast, and folks had only minutes to gather a lifetime of belongings and move to higher ground.

August, 1940
Sunday Evening

Dear Mamma,
I guess you've heard about the flood we've had. Oh, Mamma, it is the awfulest thing I've ever seen. Everything we've got is ruined. Water was nearly five feet deep in the house and mud about one foot deep all over it. We've got the floors clean, but they're humped awful. I don't know whether it can be fixed or not. My couch has mud all over it, and my bedroom suit is ruined.

The Flood of 1940

Home Cash Store

$4000 dollars to put him back in business. Five houses here in Whittier have washed away and gone. People are crossing the river in small boats. The doctors are making everybody take typhoid vaccine. Joyce and me took it this morning. I'm afraid it's going to make Joyce sick. She acts sick.

The coal house turned over and tore all to pieces. Water went everywhere! Poor old Grandma just cries and worries like everyone else.

The Red Cross has given me a mattress and two blankets. Anything you can do without, I'll be glad to get. We're in a pitiful shape and the place is completely ruined. Mud is about two feet deep all over the yard and you can't tell grass has been there.

Uncle Thad is ruined too. He said it would take

I wish you and Dad would come over as quick as you can. Joyce and me are staying at Reed's, but we hope to get back home by the middle of the week. We

My Mountain Granny

were ruined over with river water and it has got to be cleaned out. Julius went to work last night and won't come in until tomorrow. We're having to hire people to help me and I've worked until I'm nearly dead. Julius and me waded water waist deep in the house but couldn't get anything out. So if you can, I'd like for you to come. Joyce and me may have to go over there and stay awhile. I don't know what we're going to do. I'll hush for I'm tired to death.

Come if you can!

With love, Evelyn

Chapter 20
WORLD WAR II

I belong to a new generation of Americans, those born after Vietnam. I was born in "Good Times," as Evelyn often said. There has been little to fight for and certainly nothing that pulled the nation together, as the Depression or World War II did in Evelyn's time.

If you were to walk into a school classroom today, and ask a group of students what a ration consisted of, few could tell you the meaning of the word. Your chances of finding someone who had experienced rationing, are as great as getting a proper answer to the meaning of a victory garden.

Most certainly, victory gardens and war rationing are subjects sure to stir the memory of the World War II generation. In January of 1942, the office of Price Administration re-introduced rationing. In time, ten rationing programs were introduced.

Food rationing officially began on May 5, 1942, and went on to include butter, lard , coffee, sugar and red meat. Sugar was one of the first items to be rationed. These occurred due to the loss of cane fields and because ships, ordinarily used to transport sugar were used for wartime materials. The sugar book became the legal way to obtain sugar. Meat rationing went into effect in early 1943 with stamps needed to purchase sausage, hot dogs, bologna, and poultry.

The government started the national victory garden program in December of 1941. Two years later, there were nearly twenty million victory gardens producing a third of all vegetables raised in

the United States. Store owners were encouraged to close at noon on Wednesday so everyone could go home to tend their gardens.

I have enjoyed the "Good Times" of my generation, but I also know that adversity builds character. The World War II generation suffered great sacrifice but clung together to help make our nation what it is today. History is an excellent teacher, and I believe there is much to be learned from what is often called "The Greatest Generation."

Daddy's Girl

He never went overseas. Wayne Caldwell, who grew up with him, left out the same day that he did. He was first stationed down in South Carolina.

Evelyn, what was happening in Whittier as World War II began?

"We had that Depression and the big flood. After that, they called my husband to war. Julius shipped out with a bunch that left from Sylva to Ft. Bragg. He was a mechanic in the motor pool because he was too old to do anything else.

Letter to Texas

"The post mistress had to deliver "missing-in-action" letters coming in each day. The mail tripled because all the boys were overseas, and people were writing them. We'd all be down there working like crazy. There were a lot of funerals. Joyce was what kept me going. I had to take care of her and I had to train her. The day Julius left to go into WWII was right in the very worst of the war. I didn't cry, but I never had such low feelings in my life. Julius took everything with him. I had no hope he'd ever be back. I thought, 'Well, Joyce is little but I can raise her.' I had my mind made up, but he came back. It was late at night when I heard the squeak of brakes on the bus, and I knew that he was home.

"When they called Julius to the war, I drew eighty dollars a month. If I hadn't worked, I couldn't have made it. Joyce was little, and she had bronchial asthma. There were no doctors. I had to hunt a doctor to take her to. I had the awfulest time during the war. When Julius came back, Joyce was in the 2nd grade. She hadn't gone to school a day when he left. After Julius came home, he was down in the lower yard one day I was in the house. I don't remember what I was doing, but she was down there with him. I had the yard fenced in, but she had found her a little scuttle hole. She loved to go over to Reid's, which was just across the road from us a little way. Naturally, Joyce wanted to be with children, and I let her get by with a lot of slipping off. I let her get by with it because it wasn't a main highway. It was just a gravel road then.

"She started around her little post, and Julius

said, 'Joyce, come back here.' Lord, she flew so mad. She wasn't used to him controlling her—she had forgotten all about him. I'll never forget how she looked. She came in the kitchen with her eyes just a'dancing. She said, 'Mama, Mama, we was just getting along good till he came back here.'

"I thought, 'Oh law, I got to see about this.' I told Julius, 'You're gonna have to go easy with her. She's not used to your controlling her, and she's resenting you.'

"He worked into it real easy, and she was the biggest fool ever was over her daddy. He'd look at me and say, 'Evelyn, she needs tending to.' She'd fire up big-fashioned some times, but Joyce wasn't afraid of him one bit.

"Everyone in Whittier petted her. She roamed with them youngin's. They had playhouses behind the stores...that's where she was raised. John Revis was one of the best men that ever was. They'd be in their

My Mountain Granny

playhouses, and he'd send someone from the store down there with drinks. Well, Lord, they didn't have a nickel or dime. He'd give something and wouldn't charge them.

"I worked a little while in the lunchroom at school. Then I worked at the post office, and I worked at the Home Cash Store. I was always in the public.

"They wasn't too many women working. I just had one child, and I could easily do it. My husband was away all the time.

"During the war, there wasn't any meat and I got some hot dogs. Lord, I was tickled to death. I had them on the stove, and somebody came. I had company and somebody had come out on the front porch. My nephew, who was my sister's little boy, was about three or four. It never dawned on me what he'd do. He got every one of them out the pan and eat them one at a time. He was starving for meat, too. He got up in my lap and acted like he was chewing tobacco, but I knew it wasn't that. I thought, 'What's Johnny doing?'

What was the happiest time in your life?

"The happiest time was when the war was over,

104

and my husband came home. That took everything off of me. He had been gone, and I couldn't depend on him for a thing.

"We had just lived through the Depression, then the flood, and right on the heels of that they took Julius to the war. That was what my youth was made of. I just went through it all, but it was rough times. I look back on my youth, and it was a happy time. How could it not be?"

Chapter 21
IN REMEMBRANCE

The time in which I knew Evelyn was really short. I met her on December 10, 1998, and visited her off and on until her death in 2002. Evelyn was an amazing person who had lived an amazing life. Looking back on it, it's really incredible what I learned from her in the space of three years and 20 visits to her house. She often mentioned her granddaughter, Jennie Kendrick, and the time they had together.

Jennie spent much of her life with her granny and was influenced greatly by her. Her are some things Jennie remembered about her granny.

"I transferred to Myrtle Beach, SC, in 1992. Of course, Granny wanted to come and visit me. She and her friend, George-Anna Carter, came down for a week. George-Anna, who was from Miami, Florida, always went swimming in the bay at home every day. She suggested a trip to the beach. Granny declared she did not have a bathing suit. I loaned her an older one of mine, which was white and purple with flowers on it. George-Anna and I just put wraps on over our bathing suits and we were ready to hit the beach.

"Granny motioned for us to walk up the beach and back, and by then she would be ready. We ambled up the beach, deep in conversation. We turned around and walked back down in the surf, enjoying the warm water. The closer we got to where Granny had been, the more puzzled I became. I saw Granny standing in the surf, but I did not remember my bathing suit having that much white on it. I saw people pointing to her and laughing.

"Then I saw why. Granny had left her bra and panties on underneath the bathing suit. Also, she had her knee socks on out in the surf. I ran to her and told her to get rid of the underclothes, and she said, 'Well, then I would be half naked!' I asked her why on earth she had on her socks. She told me she had gotten

My Mountain Granny

stung by a jellyfish once, and she was not taking any chances of that happening again!!"

" I remember when I was about ten years old, and looking back, my grandmother would have been the age I am now (fifty). I used to live for Fridays to come because I would catch a ride with Clayton Davis, who worked at the phone company. He was married to my granny's sister, Edna. He would give me a ride to the Whittier Grocery and deposit me off with my little pink suitcase to the care of my Papa Beck. I would play store and visit people in Whittier until closing time. I would always call my Granny the moment I got to the store.

"Every Friday, it was the same ritual. She would ask me what I wanted for supper. I would say cabbage and noodles, fried potatoes, pinto beans, and corn- bread. Makes my mouth water just to think on this!!! We would have this every Friday!!! Granny used to tell me over and over that the cabbage and noodles had to be cooked separately and salted and peppered and then mixed together for the flavor to be really good. She would always surprise me with a dessert of home- made apple fritters. Since she and Papa had a lot of apple trees, I grew up on apple this and apple that and

I know an apple a day keeps the doctor away!

"After supper, she would fill two tubs up with water. One held soap water, and one was scalding hot water. We did the dishes together while Papa watched the news. Then she would ask me what book I brought to read, and we would go to the living room. She and Papa had recliners, and I sat on the couch next to the telephone. I thought I was a 'big girl' answering the phone for them. We would read until time for Jeopardy (which my grandfather would not miss). I remember Granny did not have a shower, and I always took a bath on Friday night. She had a bed light which I could use while I lay in bed and read.

"She would always come in my bedroom and tell me a Bible story and answer any questions I had. She lived by the common-sense rule. If you think something is bad or bad for you, it usually is. She used to tell me to surround myself with things I loved. To this day, I can hear her say, 'Sis, just use your com- mon sense, and God will do the rest.' Thank you, Granny, for words of wisdom!

"Granny was so happy! She had just gotten herself a brand spanking new white Mustang...I was happy too...She let me put the automatic with the gear shift in the floor into all the gears. I got to put it in reverse and drive, and we even experimented with drive one and drive two (which were lower gears to be used on mountainous terrain).

"We were going for a test drive. We got into the car which was parked in the garage and took in the newness of this spectacular machine. We tested the radio and the wipers. Then I looked over at Granny and said, 'Fireball her out of here Granny!' And that she did, right into my dad's Plymouth. He came running to see what the loud noise was and found both of us surveying the wreckage. Granny looked at my dad and said, 'Well, Jennie told me to fireball her out of there!' My dad retorted, 'Since when do you listen to an eight-year-old?' From then on when we got into our vehicles we would always say, FIREBALL HER OUT OF HERE!

"Three things I learned from my grandmother...I learned so much! It is funny how, at the age of fifty ,you think Granny was so wise, but your thoughts were much different at the age of twenty. One thing I learned from Granny is a saying I use quite often now in my church life. She always said being a Christian was just common sense. I can still hear her saying, 'Sis, if you know and feel something is wrong, it usually is. You know the Ten Commandments, and they are a good rule to live by. And also, a little drink never hurt anyone. If you rule the drinking, instead of it ruling you, then you will be okay.'

"She also taught me to surround myself with people and things I love. She said to never put the good china in a drawer to use on special occasions but to make every day a special occasion.

"Today I look at my cluttered house filled with things that are special to me (my doll collection, my dad's birdhouses he made, a carousel my dad gave his mother, a perfume collection my granny left me, all my crafts my Mom experimented with), and I have to smile because I am indeed surrounding myself with things I love and cherish. Granny also told me many, many times to be independent and to march to the beat of my own drum.

"She told me she grew up in the Depression, and she had to know how to stretch a dollar. She told me to always be where I never had to depend on someone else for anything and that meant money, happiness, and upkeep. I can still hear her saying, 'Speak your

My Mountain Granny

mind, Sis, and let the chips fall where they may.'

"Today I state my boundaries quite firmly, and most of the chips are potato chips, but I am indeed a person who marches to the beat of her own drum (whose music is my Granny's words over and over in my head). Thank God for the blessing of my granny and her words of wisdom!

Chapter 22

GOING HOME

At this time in my life, I do not have many regrets. I guess I have done as well as I possibly could. I've always believed in the Lord and went to church. I've never done no big wrong thing. I married young, and my husband and me lived together sixty-two years. I married at seventeen and the neighbors all said that we wouldn't last six months. We proved them wrong. No one thought it would work cause he was older that me.

"I never have been sorry. He was a good man and I loved him. He was the biggest fool over Joyce. He thought there wasn't anything in the world like her. I can just see him, pointing his finger. He'd say, 'I'll whip you in 30 minutes,' but he never did whip her. We've never talked about his death. One Sunday evening not long ago, we had been somewhere. Claude was driving, and he come by and turned off at the cemetery. I thought 'Oh Lord, I wish you wouldn't go there.'

"That was the first time Joyce and I had been to the cemetery since he died. She has her way, and I have my way. I just don't talk with her about him dying.

"I like to think about different scenes of my life as if I'm turning a kaleidoscope with an endless variety of patterns. I feel sad looking at photographs of my friends and family. Many of them are gone. I'm in my eighties now and a survivor. I love the Smoky Mountains, and I don't want to live anywhere else. I've had a good life and a happy one. I've always enjoyed the people that have crossed my path. I guess I'll go on reminiscing about it until the day I die."

—Evelyn Beck

During the time that I visited Evelyn, I'd get busy and go a few months without visiting. I would

My Mountain Granny

call her and the first thing she would say was, "Well, what in the world has happened to you? I've missed you." I'd then go for a visit, ashamed that I'd disappeared.

When I visited Evelyn in September Of 2001, I had been gone for awhile. Evelyn seemed well, but just before I left, she told me that her daughter had arranged to get her a room at the nursing home in Sylva.

This was a surprise. Although Evelyn was in her 80's, she still volunteered at the hospital, drove her car, and did as she pleased. I now realize that what I was seeing was not Evelyn's physical strength but her inner strength. She seemed healthy because she was always smiling and happy, regardless of how she felt.

Evelyn was independent and didn't want to leave her home but true to one of the "lessons" she taught me, she had accepted what had to be and was ready to move on.

Shortly after Christmas, I began visiting Evelyn at the nursing home. She was no longer lonely there because she had friends all around with whom she could get acquainted. Evelyn made her new room seem like home. My visits there were usually shorter

110

than when I had visited her at home.

One of my last visits with Evelyn took place a couple of weeks before her death. I got up to leave and she walked out with me. When we reached the hall she put her arm around my back as we walked through the lobby. The place was full of people sitting around, passing time and watching. All eyes were on us as we walked arm-in-arm. It must have looked like the prom king and queen walking their victory lap. I can still feel her arm around me as it was then. We hugged, and I headed off into the night.

On a Thursday evening as we were sitting down for supper my phone rang. It was Evelyn's daughter, Joyce. After talking for a short time, my wife hung up the phone. "Honey, Evelyn's had a heart attack. I think we had better go."

We drove to Sylva the next day to see her, stopping along the way to get her a card. I wasn't sure what to write but out of my pen came....

You've survived
The Great Depression
The Flood of 1940
And World War II

Going Home

You're a strong mountain woman
and you can make it

When I gave Evelyn her card, she opened it and read it aloud. She grinned and thanked me. The four of us, Evelyn, Joyce, my wife Deloris, and myself, sat and talked for an hour or so. Evelyn seemed weary, so we got up and exchanged hugs. I recall her waving goodbye as I walked around the corner. "Come back and see me. Bring your little wife with you," she said.

Sunday morning we were getting ready to go to church and the phone rang. Deloris talked for only a moment and hung up the phone. She walked over and put her hand on my shoulder. " Evelyn died this morning and Joyce wants you to be a pallbearer."

Evelyn often said that the content of her youth was the Great Depression, the Flood of 1940, and World War II. Her life was filled with hardship, but she had no regrets. The true measure of a life is not material gain, but the legacy one leaves for their family and friends. We could all do well to learn from the life of "My Mountain Granny."

Everyone whose path she crossed came away with a memory and a friend. She was smiling and laughing, never losing faith till she left us for Heaven.

Life is a Journey
When the Lord wound the hands of time,
He knew life's journey would be long,
So he created friends
To make the path smoother.
Many come and go,
But once in a lifetime,
God sends us a friend so special
She brightens our world
With the light of her love.
May we all be such a person as
Evelyn Beck was to me....

EPILOGUE

I met Evelyn Beck on December 10,1998. Only a writer can comprehend the madness that writing a book carries. The last 11 years have been filled with late nights and red eyes, crumpled paper, four letter words, and shouts of joy. My pain is now your privilege as you read the story of "My Mountain Granny."

Many times over the years I wanted to start a fire with the manuscript, but I guess I felt that I owed Evelyn something. She took me into her home, listened countless hours to my questions and made a practice of having a sandwich ready when I walked in. She opened her heart to me and told me the story of her life. Evelyn hadn't told her story until I walked in the door. It is now my job and privilege to pass it on.

What made Evelyn Beck special? She was wise yet

didn't hold a degree. Her speech was very plain spoken and country. She lived in a little country home and her possessions were very modest. Her prized possessions were pictures of her family and her well worn Bible. The things that stood out about her were not what the world today associates with success and importance. There lies the answer.

Evelyn's world as a youngster was extremely different from the one we know today. She came of age

Epilogue

when the country was steeped in the old American tradition of faith, family and hard work. The number one thing in Evelyn's life was her faith. It carried her though hard times that would have broken many. Her family was the source of much joy for her. Evelyn could recount stories about her daughter or grand-kids, and a big smile would come to her face.

Evelyn didn't want to be idle. She took pride in the fact that she still volunteered and could put in a day's work. She made a number of quilts. Thinking back, I believe the secret to her sanity was keeping her mind busy and off of loved ones, who were up in "Glory land."

Evelyn was raised to be a strong Christian woman, to take care of her family and to work hard. She lived her raising throughout her days, and that is why she lasted. Had she not held fast, the hardships she had encountered may have broken her many years before I met her.

The Bible speaks of being "A Light unto the World." Evelyn was a light to all those who knew her, and certainly to a young twenty-five-year old who came full of questions eleven years ago. I needed some light in my world, and I found it when I knocked on her door. The lessons I learned from Evelyn will remain with me the rest of my years.

To Order Additional Books

Please contact the author at the following email address:

Matthew Baker

Email: mattdeloris@smnet.net